Praise for *Adjudicating Construction and Engineering Disputes*

'A great judge once wrote: "The life of the law has not been logic: it has been experience." *Adjudicating Construction and Engineering Disputes* brings together the vast experience of two of the UK's most prominent adjudicators. For the neophyte adjudicator as well as the old hand, there is a richness of practical wisdom in this book for decision makers to mine".

— **Julian Bailey**, Partner, Jones Day and author of *Construction Law* (4th edition)

'This book will become the definitive guide for adjudicators not only in the UK but in all jurisdictions that adopt this method of dispute resolution. It is practical yet rigorous, concise yet comprehensive. The appendices are likely to be of great assistance. We are lucky that Jonathan Cope and Matthew Molloy have shared their extraordinary expertise and insightful advice with us.'

— **Professor Renato Nazzini PhD FCIArb**, director of the Centre of Construction Law and Dispute Resolution, King's College London

'This book is an invaluable guide to adjudication. Written from the adjudicator's perspective, in an accessible and fluent style, it is full of very useful and practical information gleaned from the authors' many years of experience. Everyone will learn from this book. I highly recommend it.'

— **Victoria Russell LLB FCIArb FCIOB FFB**, honorary president of the Adjudication Society

'Clear, practical, easy to follow and comprehensive, this start-to-finish guide to adjudication applies internationally. Matthew Molloy and Jonathan Cope have got the balance right, for practitioners and party representatives alike. They do not overwhelm with academic detail, but everything you need to know is there, clearly informed by the authors' decades of real-world experience.'

— **Dr John Fletcher**, Executive Director, Dispute Resolution Service, RICS

'Molloy and Cope's book provides a solid "cradle to grave" practical guide to those who wish to practise or are already practising as adjudicators of construction and engineering disputes. The subject matter of the book, although primarily focused on adjudication practice in the UK, is also applicable internationally in jurisdictions where adjudication legislation has been enacted or where there are adjudication provisions within the contract. Molloy and Cope emphasize the common features of adjudication within each jurisdiction: for example, while the substantive laws do differ between jurisdictions, the common principles are that there must be a dispute, the adjudicator's Decision is temporarily binding, natural justice should be adhered to in relation to procedural fairness and the adjudicator having to act impartially and/or independent of the parties, and Decisions should be reached within a prescribed time limit. Molloy and Cope also broadly identify the differences between each jurisdiction. The book does a very good job of providing a practical guide to the practice of adjudication from the perspective of an adjudicator.'

— **Robert Gemmell LLM FRICS FCIArb**, Chartered Arbitrator

ADJUDICATING CONSTRUCTION AND ENGINEERING DISPUTES

ADJUDICATING CONSTRUCTION AND ENGINEERING DISPUTES

Matthew Molloy and Jonathan Cope

LONDON PUBLISHING PARTNERSHIP

Published by London Publishing Partnership
www.londonpublishingpartnership.co.uk

ISBN: 978-1-916749-27-6 (hbk)
ISBN: 978-1-916749-28-3 (iPDF)
ISBN: 978-1-916749-29-0 (epub)

A catalogue record for this book is
available from the British Library

This book has been composed in
Adobe Garamond Pro

Copy-edited and typeset by
T&T Productions Ltd, London
www.tandtproductions.com

Cover designed by Fold7
https://fold7.com/

To our mums, Maureen and Twink,
and our dads, Tom and Peter

Contents

Foreword

When I was preparing the first edition of *Coulson on Construction Adjudication*, I thought that, at the end of the book, after all that law, it would be a good idea to have a practical guide to adjudication. This would set out what was involved in this new process of dispute resolution, and what an adjudicator should do – and sometimes not do – to run an adjudication properly. It has always been a part of the book that readers have liked and commented positively about.

That may well be because that section was primarily not written by me, but by Matt Molloy. I chose Matt because, even fifteen years ago, he was one of the best known and most practically minded of all the construction professionals undertaking adjudication work. His partnership with Jonathan Cope in MCMS Ltd, now further cemented by the production of this book, makes them a veritable powerhouse in the world of construction adjudication.

Of course, one of the things that this book will do is render the last part of my own completely otiose. That is because what this book does is to take that idea as a starting point, but then expand it into a detailed, thoughtful and user-friendly guide to every aspect of construction adjudication. Although both Matt and Jonathan are knowledgeable lawyers, the law is kept in the background, brought out to emphasize a particular point, but otherwise properly kept on a very short leash.

Instead, the book tells adjudicators, and those who practise in this field, how a successful adjudication should be run, the sensible steps to take at every stage and the traps to avoid. What is even more astonishing is that, as the book's introduction makes clear, this guidance will apply not just in England and Wales but to all the jurisdictions around the world – and they are many – that have embraced construction adjudication. It is of international application, which is quite an achievement.

Although this is emphatically not a legal textbook – it might be said to be much too useful to be that – I look forward to the first time that it is cited to me in the Court of Appeal. And I am confident it will be!

I wish it every success.

Sir Peter Coulson
Royal Courts of Justice
May 2024

Preface

The purpose of this book is to provide a practical guide to those who either wish to practise or are already practising as adjudicators of construction and engineering disputes.

Although the authors' practice developed as a direct result of the introduction of a statutory adjudication regime in the United Kingdom that was enacted in 1998,[1] the book is not intended to be jurisdiction specific. This is in recognition of the prevalence of, and increase in, the use of adjudication as a mechanism for dealing with disputes that arise under and in connection with construction and engineering contracts worldwide. This is as a result either of legislation enacted or pending in other jurisdictions, e.g. Ireland, Australia, New Zealand, Malaysia, Mauritius, Singapore, Hong Kong, South Africa and Canada, or of provisions within standard form and bespoke contracts between parties from either the same or different countries, e.g. the FIDIC Conditions of Contract. At the time of drafting the book, the International Statutory Adjudication Forum has also drafted and circulated a 'Model Law on Statutory Adjudication' for consultation.

When the authors set out on their endeavour to practise as adjudicators in the late 1990s and early 2000s there was little by way of practical guidance. The training that was available was generally directed towards those who had already had some exposure to, or training in, arbitration. It was therefore limited in duration, and the content was focused on the applicable procedural rules or statutory framework. Since that time more extensive courses have been made available, such as those offered by the Royal Institution of Chartered Surveyors and the Chartered Institute of Arbitrators and their affiliates, as have modules dedicated to adjudication law and practice and Decision writing included

1 The Housing Grants, Construction and Regeneration Act 1996.

within postgraduate courses on construction law and dispute resolution. However, although there are now more texts available on the subject of adjudication, many of which seek to draw on the growing body of case law across the world, there is relatively little by way of a guide to the practice of adjudication from the perspective of an adjudicator. It is hoped that this book will go some way to filling that void and help those who are considering practising as an adjudicator or who are pursuing a qualification that encompasses the practice of adjudication.

As a consequence of its wider focus, this book does not attempt to cover the jurisprudence or law in relation to adjudication in any great depth. However, as the fundamental principles of procedural fairness and the mechanics of reaching and writing a Decision are common across jurisdictions, the book does draw on examples where the conduct of adjudicators has been the subject of judicial comment in order to highlight what has been considered to represent good or bad practice. Readers should note that the main source of the limited adjudication case law that we refer to is from the United Kingdom, and it should be emphasized that what is deemed appropriate in one jurisdiction may not reflect the position in other jurisdictions.

For an in-depth analysis of the law of adjudication in the United Kingdom, we would recommend that readers refer to the relevant practitioner texts, the leading one of which is *Coulson on Construction Adjudication*.[2] For those readers interested in the law of adjudication in different jurisdictions, we would recommend that reference is made to the relevant chapters of *Construction Law*.[3]

---

2 Rt. Hon. Lord Justice Coulson. 2018. *Coulson on Construction Adjudication*, 4th edition. Oxford University Press.

3 Julian Bailey. 2024. *Construction Law*, 4th edition. London Publishing Partnership.

Acknowledgments

Without wishing to come across like an Academy Award acceptance speech, there are many people we need to thank for their help and support in the production of this book. First and foremost, thank you to our publishers, Sam and Richard at London Publishing Partnership, for their expert guidance over the past two years, as well as for their endless patience during the editorial process. Credit for the excellent cover has to go to Ryan Newey and Alex Gill at Fold7 – we are very grateful for their creativity.

Thank you to Sir Peter Coulson, not only for his wonderful foreword but more generally for his support for adjudication. Without that support, and that of other senior members of the judiciary before him, we are sure that adjudication would been considerably less successful than it has been in the United Kingdom and beyond.

Thank you to Victoria Russell and Julian Bailey for peer reviewing the book, and to Julian in particular for his comments on adjudication in some of the jurisdictions with which we are less familiar. Robert Gemmell was also very helpful in dispensing wisdom about adjudication in the Australian states, and thanks too to Murray Armes and Stacy Sinclair for their input on three-person tribunals and artificial intelligence, respectively. We are also grateful to Professor Renato Nazzini and Dr John Fletcher for taking time out from their busy schedules to review the book.

We have shared our experiences of writing Decisions, and we have stressed the importance of having them proofread. The vast majority of our Decisions have been proofread by our amazing practice manager, Helena Riches, and it would be remiss of us not to thank her for all her hard work over the past twenty years. Without Helena, howlers such as 'cheery pickers' (rather than 'cherry pickers') would probably have made it into our Decisions! Other colleagues that deserve a special mention are Liz Stephens, who keeps our office running like a tight ship, and Cassie Leaver, who has been instrumental in launching this book.

Last, but by no means least, thanks to our families. To our wives, Helen and Theresa, who made us believe in ourselves – without their love and support, this book would never have got written. Thanks must also go to our children, Megan, Patrick, Zelda, Leo, Gabriella and Jemima, for their inspiration and for keeping our feet on the ground.

CHAPTER 1

Introduction

This book is intended as a walk through from the beginning to the end of an adjudicator's involvement with a dispute arising under or in connection with a construction or engineering contract, i.e. a 'cradle to grave' guide. This introductory chapter seeks to provide some context to construction industry adjudication, covering the historical background and the field's development, the differences between statutory and contractual adjudication, and the differences between domestic and international adjudication models. It also sets out what we consider to be the key principles that are common to the different processes and explains the different approach taken by certain jurisdictions as to the type of dispute that can be referred to adjudication.

The following chapters then proceed chronologically, covering initial steps and the appointment stage, initial directions, procedural and case management considerations, dealing with objections to jurisdiction, managing submissions and evidence, conducting meetings/hearings and site inspections, dealing with different types of parties and disputes, identifying issues, drafting and presenting the Decision, and addressing any post-Decision issues that may arise. Within these substantive chapters we also provide some examples based on our experience of practising as adjudicators.

Our first appendix is about how to become an adjudicator, covering the typical academic and vocational requirements, how to get that elusive first appointment, and developing a practice as an adjudicator. The remaining appendices include example documents, including an example Decision, which we hope will helpfully illustrate some of what we have said in this book.

THE HISTORICAL CONTEXT AND BACKGROUND TO ADJUDICATION

Although there are some older examples of adjudication provisions in construction contracts, for present purposes we consider that the best starting point is the United Kingdom and the enactment of the Housing Grants, Construction and Regeneration Act 1996 ('the UK Construction Act'), which came into force in May 1998. We say this because, as far as we are aware, the Act was the first legislation anywhere in the world to introduce a statutory right for parties to a construction contract (as defined by the legislation) to refer a dispute to adjudication. It has also been the catalyst for other jurisdictions across the world to introduce their own statutory legislation, as well as providing a developed body of case law providing guidance as to how adjudication can work in practice and how adjudicators should conduct themselves. However, we would repeat the point made in the preface that what is deemed appropriate in one jurisdiction, and specifically in the United Kingdom, might not be appropriate in other jurisdictions. This is especially so in the context of what type of dispute can be the subject of an adjudication and also what arguments can be relied upon by the parties.

The introduction of the UK Construction Act was the product of lobbying on the part of certain sectors of the construction industry to address concerns regarding the adversarial nature of the industry and the expense and time associated with resolving disputes. There was a perception that the balance of power lay with those who had greater financial strength, as they could dictate terms and defer or delay payment to the supply chain. A party could wait years after a project had completed to receive payment, assuming that they had the means to pursue their entitlement through the courts or arbitration. Construction contracts would often defer the right to refer disputes until after the defects rectification period had expired and/or was signed off by a certifier. Main contractors would often pass down these provisions such that subcontractors whose work had long been completed had little means of obtaining access to justice without delay. Similarly, main contractors would typically include 'paid when paid' provisions in their subcontracts in order to transfer risk.

Assuming that a party had the means to pursue a claim by referring the dispute to court or arbitration, it would often have to wait many years before having its claim heard. Although there was a specialist division of the High Court in England & Wales that dealt with construction industry cases (the Official Referees), it was a limited resource: it had a long waiting list to have cases heard and it required the instruction of specialist lawyers (with rights of audience) and experts. Trials could be long, as could the wait for a judgment. The alternative was arbitration – anecdotally referred to by some as 'litigation in suits' – which could often also be a lengthy and expensive process. Recalcitrant or reluctant parties could delay proceedings by lodging objections to jurisdiction, by applying for security for costs, by insisting on a lengthy disclosure procedure, and by forcing a hearing that – apart from the fact counsel and the judge were not wigged and gowned – replicated a hearing in the High Court.

In 1993 the UK government appointed Sir Michael Latham, a former MP, to undertake a review of procurement and contractual arrangements, and a report entitled *Constructing the Team* was produced the following year.[1] Sir Michael summed up the payment problems at the time as follows:

> 'This disturbing atmosphere was summed up for me by a medium-sized specialist contractor … who said bluntly that "there is no trust at all in the industry any more". It was repeated by a large international main contractor who said that if he was treated fairly by clients and able to make a reasonable profit, he would respond appropriately and give his client a good deal. He felt that many of the difficulties which currently beset the industry would then simply disappear. Too little trust – and not enough money. A mighty machine which requires oil in its engine to drive it has grit instead.'

There were two facets to the UK Construction Act. As well as introducing the right to refer a dispute to adjudication, it also imposed mandatory payment provisions. The payment provisions included a prohibition on 'paid when paid' clauses (save for on the grounds of insolvency up the supply chain, and even then subject to a contract providing for such circumstances) and introduced a payment notice regime whereby paying parties were obliged to give details of what they were paying and explain why they were withholding sums. These provisions were then subject to amendment and were strengthened in 2011 (as a result of the Local Democracy, Economic Development and Construction Act 2009) with provision being made, under certain circumstances, for a payer to be obliged to pay a sum

1 *Constructing the Team*. 1994. See https://en.wikipedia.org/wiki/Latham_Report.

claimed in full in the event it did not comply with its obligation to serve a timely and sufficiently detailed payment notice.

Allied to the payment provisions were the mandatory adjudication provisions. To the extent a construction contract (as defined) did not comply with the UK Construction Act, the applicable provisions of secondary legislation would apply: namely, the Scheme for Construction Contracts ((England & Wales), (Scotland) or (Northern Ireland) as applicable) Regulations 1998. Key features of the mandatory adjudication provisions were that qualifying contracts must provide for either party to be able to unilaterally refer a dispute to an adjudicator at any time, and that the adjudicator would have an obligation to reach a Decision within 28 days of the dispute being referred. The 28-day timetable could be extended to 42 days by the applicant (commonly known as the Referring Party) or to an even longer period if both parties agreed. The Decision of the adjudicator was to be temporarily binding on the parties such that the parties would be obliged to comply with it in the first instance. Although it might be possible to resist the enforcement of a Decision on certain limited grounds, this would not be by way of an appeal. Assuming that a Decision was enforceable and that one or both parties did not agree with it, the disgruntled party could subsequently refer the dispute to the courts or to arbitration to have the matter determined afresh.

OTHER STATUTORY SCHEMES

At the time of writing, the following jurisdictions have enacted legislation that provides for the right to refer disputes in relation to construction contracts to adjudication:

(i) Australia

- (a) New South Wales[2]
- (b) Queensland[3]
- (c) Victoria[4]
- (d) Tasmania[5]

---

2 Building and Construction Industry Security of Payment Act 1999 (NSW).

3 Building Industry Fairness (Security of Payment) Act 2017 (Qld), which superseded the Building and Construction Industry Security of Payment Act 2004 (Qld).

4 Building and Construction Industry Security of Payment Act 2002 (Vic).

5 Building and Construction Industry Security of Payment Act 2009 (Tas).

(e) Australian Capital Territory[6]
(f) South Australia[7]
(g) Western Australia[8]
(h) The Northern Territory[9]

(ii) New Zealand[10]

(iii) Malaysia[11]

(iv) Singapore[12]

(v) Ireland[13]

(vi) Canada

(a) Ontario[14]
(b) Saskatchewan[15]
(c) Alberta[16]
(d) New Brunswick[17]
(e) Quebec (pilot) [18]

---

6 Building and Construction Industry (Security of Payment) Act 2009 (ACT).

7 Building and Construction Industry Security of Payment Act 2009 (SA).

8 Building and Construction Industry (Security of Payment) Act 2021 (WA).

9 Construction Contracts (Security of Payments) Act 2004 (NT).

10 Construction Contract Act 2002 (NZ), as amended by the Construction Contracts Amendment Act 2015 and the Construction Contracts (Retention Money) Amendment Act 2023 (NZ).

11 Construction Industry Payment and Adjudication Act 2012.

12 Building and Construction Industry Security of Payment Act (2004) (Sing), as amended by the Building and Construction Industry Security of Payment (Amendment) Act (Cap 47, 2018).

13 Construction Contracts Act 2013.

14 Construction Act, R.S.O. 1990, c. 30, Part II.1 (Ontario).

15 The Builders' Lien Act, SS 1984-85-86, c. B-7.1 (Saskatchewan).

16 Prompt Payment and Construction Lien Act, RSA 2000, c. B-7, Part 5 (Alberta).

17 Construction Prompt Payment and Adjudication Act, SNB 2023, c. 15, Part 3 (New Brunswick).

18 Bill 12: an Act mainly to promote Québec-sourced and responsible procurement by public bodies, to reinforce the integrity regime of enterprises, and to increase the powers of the Autorité des marchés publics (enacted on 2 June 2022).

(f) Federal[19]
(g) Manitoba[20]

(vii) The Isle of Man[21]

The following jurisdictions have either drafted legislation, have legislation pending, or are discussing proposals to introduce the right to refer disputes arising under construction contracts to adjudication:

(i) Canada

(a) Nova Scotia[22]
(b) British Columbia[23]

(ii) Hong Kong[24]

(iii) Mauritius[25]

(iv) South Africa[26]

(v) Thailand[27]

---

19 Federal Prompt Payment for Construction Work Act (S.C. 2019, c. 29, s. 387).

20 The Builders' Liens Amendment Act (Prompt Payment) received royal assent on 30 May 2023.

21 Construction Contracts Act 2004.

22 An Act to amend Chapter 277 of the Revised Statutes, 1989 – the Builders' Lien Act – received royal assent.

23 Report on The Builders Lien Act published in July 2020.

24 The Construction Industry Security of Payment Ordinance, which will introduce adjudication, is currently forecast to be introduced in 2025.

25 Construction Contracts Act 2016 (discussion draft).

26 The Construction Industry Development Board Act, 2000 (Act 38 of 2000) imposes a mandatory standard for state bodies.

27 A draft bill on 'Act on Settlement of Disputes relating to Payment under Construction Contracts' has been published for consultation.

A common feature of the various statutory adjudication regimes that are either in force or contemplated in the above jurisdictions is the coincidence of the introduction of adjudication with payment legislation. This serves to highlight the link between fair and prompt payment and adjudication. The context of adjudication is therefore that it serves as a form of policing mechanism in relation to payment-related disputes whereby parties are able to refer disputes to a neutral third party for a Decision in a relatively short period of time (typically 28–30 days) that is binding in the interim. The rubric of 'pay now argue later' is sometimes used to highlight the point that parties who do not agree with an adjudicator's Decision that directs payment of a sum are nevertheless obliged to pay now, but they can argue the point again later in front of a different tribunal (such as a court or arbitrator) that is empowered to determine the dispute on a final and binding basis (subject to the relevant rights of appeal).

INTERNATIONAL/CROSS-BORDER/ NON-STATUTORY REGIMES

The most prominent form of contractual adjudication is that found in the FIDIC forms of contract. In the 1999 FIDIC forms of contract the 'adjudicator' is referred to as the Dispute Adjudication Board, or 'DAB'. In contrast to the statutory adjudication regimes (which envisage a sole adjudicator), the DAB can comprise one or three members. The DAB can also be either standing (i.e. appointed at the outset of the project and kept apprised of progress through site visits and reports and called upon to reach a Decision if one of the parties elects to refer a dispute to the DAB) or ad hoc (i.e. appointed after a dispute has arisen). The time period prescribed for a Decision is 84 days from the date of the dispute being referred to the DAB.

The 2017 forms of FIDIC contracts provide for a Dispute Avoidance and Adjudication Board (a 'DAAB'). Similar to the DAB, the DAAB can consist of one or three members. The 'avoidance' element highlights that one role of the DAAB is to assist the parties in avoiding disputes. This is additional to the adjudication function, which operates in a similar manner to the DAB in the 1999 forms of FIDIC contracts.

KEY COMMON PRINCIPLES

A common principle is that, in order for there to be a reference to adjudication, there must be a qualifying dispute. However, the question of whether a dispute 'qualifies' will be jurisdiction specific. For example, in the United Kingdom, the 'dispute' must arise under a construction contract as defined in the UK Construction Act and/or not be subject to an exemption, e.g. construction contracts with residential owner-occupiers are 'excluded' contracts.

The scope of the disputes that may be referred under the UK Construction Act is extensive. However, in Ireland, as well as defining what constitutes a construction contract, the legislation also provides that it is only 'payment disputes' that may be referred to adjudication. Other jurisdictions also restrict adjudication to payment notice disputes and/or to claims by a payee 'up the line' to the payer and not vice versa: this is the case in Queensland, for example, but not in the United Kingdom. The concept of a dispute in the United Kingdom is therefore wider than it is in other jurisdictions, which may restrict the type of dispute that may be referred.

Although the underlying substantive law may differ between jurisdictions, it is a truism that a dispute is different to a claim. For a dispute to arise, there must have been a claim or assertion by one party that is rejected or not accepted by the other. The rejection of the claim may be obvious, e.g. an express statement to that effect, or inferred, e.g. by conduct. Conduct giving rise to a dispute could include silence and/or non-payment of a sum claimed by the final date for payment of that sum.

RELEVANT CASE LAW

In the UK case of *Amec Civil Engineering Ltd v Secretary of State for Transport*,[28] Mr Justice Jackson (as he was then) derived the following principles as to the meaning of a 'dispute' (paragraph 68), which were subsequently approved by the Court of Appeal.[29]

---

28 [2004] EWHC 2339 (TCC).

29 [2005] EWCA Civ 291.

'1. The word "dispute" which occurs in many arbitration clauses and also in section 108 of the Housing Grants Act should be given its normal meaning. It does not have some special or unusual meaning conferred upon it by lawyers.
2. Despite the simple meaning of the word "dispute", there has been much litigation over the years as to whether or not disputes existed in particular situations. This litigation has not generated any hard-edged legal rules as to what is or is not a dispute. However, the accumulating judicial decisions have produced helpful guidance.
3. The mere fact that one party (whom I shall call "the claimant") notifies the other party (whom I shall call "the respondent") of a claim does not automatically and immediately give rise to a dispute. It is clear, both as a matter of language and from judicial decisions, that a dispute does not arise unless and until it emerges that the claim is not admitted.
4. The circumstances from which it may emerge that a claim is not admitted are Protean. For example, there may be an express rejection of the claim. There may be discussions between the parties from which objectively it is to be inferred that the claim is not admitted. The respondent may prevaricate, thus giving rise to the inference that he does not admit the claim. The respondent may simply remain silent for a period of time, thus giving rise to the same inference.
5. The period of time for which a respondent may remain silent before a dispute is to be inferred depends heavily upon the facts of the case and the contractual structure. Where the gist of the claim is well known and it is obviously controversial, a very short period of silence may suffice to give rise to this inference. Where the claim is notified to some agent of the respondent who has a legal duty to consider the claim independently and then give a considered response, a longer period of time may be required before it can be inferred that mere silence gives rise to a dispute.
6. If the claimant imposes upon the respondent a deadline for responding to the claim, that deadline does not have the automatic effect of curtailing what would otherwise be a reasonable time for responding. On the other hand, a stated

> deadline and the reasons for its imposition may be relevant factors when the court comes to consider what is a reasonable time for responding.
>
> 7. If the claim as presented by the claimant is so nebulous and ill-defined that the respondent cannot sensibly respond to it, neither silence by the respondent nor even an express non-admission is likely to give rise to a dispute for the purposes of arbitration or adjudication.'

Another common feature is that of the temporary finality of the adjudicator's Decision. The parties will therefore be bound by an adjudication Decision unless and until either the parties reach a final agreement or a court or arbitrator delivers a finally binding judgment or award in respect of (or encompassing) the dispute that was decided by the adjudicator.

A further common feature is the requirement of the adjudicator to act in a procedurally fair manner. This concept is sometimes referred to as due process, and it represents one of two principles of natural justice: namely, that a party to a dispute has the right to be heard (i.e. to put forward their case or position) and to be given a reasonable opportunity to respond to the opposing party's case or position. This feature needs to be considered in the context of a fast-track procedure that is not necessarily finally determinative.

Another commonality is the requirement for the adjudicator to be impartial and/or independent of the parties. This is the second of the two principles of natural justice, i.e. that no one shall be a judge in their own cause. The question of whether an adjudicator satisfies the requirement of impartiality may be resolved by reference to either a historic or current involvement with the parties or their representatives or by reference to their conduct of the adjudication itself or the treatment of the parties.

The final common feature is the requirement for a Decision to be reached within a prescribed time limit, typically between 28 and 30 days from the date the adjudicator receives the Referral. Although this time limit can be extended in certain circumstances, the main point to note is the relatively short period of time for the adjudication process when compared to arbitration or litigation. Even the period prescribed in the FIDIC forms of contract (84 days) is still relatively short. This creates challenges for the parties to an adjudication and is a key characteristic of the process that impacts both on the way adjudication is conducted and on its treatment by supervising courts.

WIDE VERSUS NARROW SCOPE

Although the question of what type of construction contracts and what type of disputes can be the subject of adjudication will depend on the applicable legislation and the specific contract, such that it will vary between jurisdictions, we consider that the type of disputes that may be referred broadly fall into two categories: namely, 'wide' or 'narrow'.

The wide category of dispute is one that is not limited by a type. An example of this is those in the United Kingdom, where the UK Construction Act specifies that a dispute (which includes 'any difference') arising under a construction contract may be referred to adjudication. Thus the type of dispute is not restricted. The Courts of England and Wales have found that, even though the UK Construction Act refers to disputes arising 'under' a construction contract, this can be construed as encompassing disputes in connection with construction contracts. Therefore, for example, it may be possible to refer claims relating to misrepresentation or rectification to adjudication under the UK regime. Further, in the United Kingdom the courts have held that the right to refer a dispute is not restricted by reference to time, such that disputes can be (and in our experience are) referred to adjudication after a project has been completed and/or after a contract has come to an end as a result of a termination.

RELEVANT CASE LAW

Relevant cases from which we derive the proposition that, at least in the United Kingdom, disputes arising in connection with a construction contract can be referred to adjudication include the following.

1. The Supreme Court's decision in *Aspect Contracts (Asbestos) Ltd v Higgins Construction Plc*.[30] In that case, Aspect argued that the principles established in *Premium Nafta Products Limited (20th Defendant) and others (Respondents) v Fili Shipping Company Limited (14th Claimant) and others (Appellants)*[31] ('the Fiona Trust case') – namely, that the construction of an arbitration clause should start from the presumption that the parties are likely to have

30 [2015] UKSC 38.
31 [2007] UKHL 40.

intended all disputes to be decided by the same tribunal – applies to adjudication clauses, therefore superseding previous authorities, including *Fillite (Runcorn) Ltd v Aqua-lift*. Lord Mance confirmed that he was content to accept Aspect's contention (paragraph 22).

2. *J Murphy & Sons Ltd v W Maher and Sons Ltd*,[32] in which Sir Robert Akenhead carefully explained why he considered that the Fiona Trust case applies to adjudication clauses. He concluded by saying (paragraph 32): 'I consider that the Courts at the highest level have strongly signposted a departure from such previous distinctions and that the Courts on adjudication cases should follow this direction [i.e. that set out in Fiona Trust case].'

3. *Paice & Anor v Harding (t/a MJ Harding Contractors)*,[33] in which Mrs Justice O'Farrell confirmed that in *Aspect* the Supreme Court 'accepted that an alternative cause of action could fall within the language of section 108(1) of the 1996 Act' (paragraph 69).

4. The Supreme Court's decision in *Bresco Electrical Services Ltd (In Liquidation) v Michael J Lonsdale (Electrical) Ltd*,[34] in which Lord Briggs stated (paragraph 41): 'I am not persuaded that the statutory compulsion lying behind the conferral of the contractual right to adjudicate points at all towards giving the phrase "a dispute arising under the contract" a narrow meaning, by comparison with a similar phrase in a contract freely negotiated. The fact that, after due consideration of the Latham Report, Parliament considered that construction adjudication was such a good thing that all parties to such contracts should have the right to go to adjudication points if anything in the opposite direction. Indeed, the fact that the right to adjudicate is statutorily guaranteed is a powerful consideration favourable both to its recognition as a matter of construction, and to the caution which the court ought to employ before preventing its exercise by injunction.'

32 [2016] EWHC 1148 (TCC).

33 [2016] EWHC 2945 (TCC).

34 [2020] UKSC 25.

A narrow category of dispute is one that is limited. Examples of this can be found in Australia and, to a lesser extent, Ireland, which restricts the right to adjudicate to payment disputes. That is not to say that a payment dispute may not encompass, say, time-related or quality matters, but it is suggested that such matters would need to be determinative or relevant to the payment dispute. In a construction context it is not too difficult for such matters to fall within the scope of a dispute regarding an entitlement to payment. For example, an entitlement to an extension of time may affect an entitlement to compensation or damages. Similarly, deductions may be levied as a result of alleged defects in the works. However, simply seeking declaratory relief as to an entitlement to an extension of time would not be permitted.

In Australia, despite there being differences in wording and applicability of legislation across the six states and two territories, a common feature is that it is a precondition to adjudication that a contractor/payee has submitted a payment claim in accordance with either the contract or relevant security of payment legislation. If a party/payer then fails to assess the sum due within a prescribed period or pay by the due date, or assesses an amount that is less than that claimed, the payee is then entitled to commence an adjudication within the time prescribed under the applicable legislation.

In the context of payment claim or security of payment disputes, there may also be restrictions on the arguments that can be advanced as a defence against non-payment. For example, in New South Wales and other jurisdictions that adopt a similar approach, such as Singapore, Malaysia and New Zealand, the legislation restricts what the adjudicator can consider and prohibits a payer from including reasons for refusing payment in its adjudication Response that could (and should) have been included in a 'payment schedule' (i.e. the payer's original assessment).

CHAPTER 2

The appointment

In this chapter we cover the pre-appointment and appointment stages of an adjudication. In relation to pre-appointment, we look at the different types of appointment that may arise and the typical considerations that a prospective adjudicator will need to account for when deciding whether to accept an appointment. Thereafter we cover the appointment itself and look at terms, initial communications and directions, as well as discussing how to deal with any initial objections to an adjudicator's appointment.

DIFFERENT TYPES OF APPOINTMENT

In broad terms there are three different types of appointment. The first is appointments received from an authorized nominating authority or institution. The second is appointments received as a result of a direct enquiry or agreement between the parties. Finally, there are appointments as a result of an adjudicator being named in a contract.

Most relevant legislation and contracts provide that parties may apply to an institution or body to appoint an adjudicator in the event the parties do not agree who and/or how an adjudicator is to be appointed. Certain jurisdictions restrict this to a sole appointing authority. For example, in Ireland appointments may be made by a panel set up by the Irish government (the 'Minister's panel'), while Canadian provinces grant licenses to a single 'adjudicator nominating authority' (ANA) within each province. In contrast, the United Kingdom allows any body that holds itself out as an appointing authority (an 'adjudicator nominating body' (ANB)) to make such appointments. As a consequence, there are a number of ANBs in the United Kingdom. Some of these have been set up by construction industry professional bodies and some by dispute resolution organizations; others are privately run organizations set up specifically for the purpose of appointing adjudicators. The UK approach is therefore effectively a 'free market' system.

The various nominating authorities will typically hold lists or rosters of adjudicators. The criteria for inclusion on these lists varies, but to be included on any list an individual will typically need to possess an underlying professional qualification, have experience of construction projects or disputes, have knowledge and understanding of construction and the law, and may also be required to possess an adjudication-specific qualification or to have attended an adjudication-specific training course. In order to be admitted or included on a list, candidates might also need to undergo some form of assessment, which might include a documentary submission and, in some instances, involve an interview. ANAs and ANBs may also levy an application fee for potential candidates.

Once admitted on a list or roster an adjudicator may also have to comply with requirements such as maintaining a prescribed level of professional indemnity insurance cover, undertaking continuous professional development (CPD), submitting to a complaints handling or disciplinary process, and paying an annual fee. Membership of panels may also be subject to reassessment at certain intervals. For example, membership of the Irish Minister's panel is currently for a fixed term of five years, while the Chartered Institute of Arbitrators issues 'panel appointment certificates' for a three-year term.

Our experience is that an adjudicator's first appointment is likely to be as a result of being included on an ANA/ANB list. This is understandable as it is unlikely that parties (or their advisors) would agree to, or name, an adjudicator who did not either have experience of conducting an adjudication or had otherwise acted in some judicial or quasi-judicial capacity, such as an arbitrator. This can sometimes lead to a chicken and egg situation whereby, to be included on a list of adjudicators, a candidate might need to demonstrate experience of adjudication and (in some instances) experience of actually having acted as adjudicator. Thankfully, some practitioners and professional bodies have set up pupillage or shadowing schemes for suitably qualified adjudicators to enable them to acquire first-hand experience of conducting an adjudication while observing an experienced adjudicator, and such experience can then be used in support of an application to be included on a list or roster. We cover the differing approaches adopted by ANAs/ANBs in respect of appointments later in this chapter. We also cover the key considerations for prospective adjudicators when receiving an enquiry from an ANA/ANB.

The second type of appointment is one where the parties agree after a dispute has arisen that a particular adjudicator should act. As already alluded to, where a party (or, more typically, their representative or advisor) has experience or knowledge of an adjudicator, they may seek to propose an individual or list of names to the other side for consideration. Although there may be some reluctance to accept or agree to an individual proposed by the other side, our experience is that, where the representatives are experienced, the fact that the other side has put forward an individual does not usually, in itself, preclude a party from accepting that individual in circumstances where they consider them to be suitable.

Our personal experience of direct appointments is that we are approached by one side either before being proposed or after the partes have agreed that we should act. When we are approached beforehand, we are typically asked to confirm our availability and also whether we have any conflicts of interest. We cover these issues later in this chapter, but for now we would make the point that it is important to record and note any enquiries made as it might be necessary to disclose the nature of the enquiry to the other side in the event the matter proceeds. This is to avoid any issue arising regarding unilateral communications with a party. Although not entirely on point, we are aware of guidance provided by the Chartered Institute of Arbitrators for arbitrators who are approached by parties, and we consider this is helpful in pointing out the pitfalls associated with unilateral contact with a party prior to an appointment.[1] For example, it would not be appropriate to discuss the details of a case or enter into dialogue as to how the adjudicator might approach an issue as this could give rise to a challenge on the grounds of procedural unfairness or perceived bias. Nowadays, most enquiries we receive are via email, which makes it easier to record and disclose any communications post appointment. However, this is not always the case, and it may be that enquiries are made via a telephone call or even

1 Chartered Institute of Arbitrators. 2015. Interviews for Prospective Arbitrators. International Arbitration Practice Guideline.

in person at an event. In such circumstances it is important to keep a note for the reasons cited.

RELEVANT CASE LAW

In the UK case of *Paice & Anor v MJ Harding (t/a MJ Harding Contractors)*,[2] Mr Justice Coulson (as he was then) refused to enforce the Decision of an adjudicator on the grounds of bias in circumstances where the adjudicator had failed to disclose his knowledge of telephone calls made to his office two months prior to the adjudication, in which the employers had spoken at length to his office manager about the dispute. Although the adjudicator had not been party to the conversations, he had actual knowledge of the content of them, which went beyond merely procedural matters.

When approached after an agreement has been reached by the parties, the key considerations are, again, availability and whether the adjudicator is free of conflicts. The enquiries of this type that we typically receive are usually subject to confirmation of our willingness to act. From a contractual perspective, as well as confirmation from the 'agreed' adjudicator that they are willing to act, the appointment may not actually be effective until terms have been proposed and accepted. It is perhaps surprising that our experience is that parties do not always ask for terms to be provided in advance of confirmation of agreement. Where terms have already been provided the position may be more straightforward, but where they have not already been provided the approach we take is to provide a copy of our terms and then to confirm that any agreement to act is subject to those terms. Those who are more cautious may seek confirmation of acceptance by the parties, but others may elect to rely on acceptance by conduct. In the case of the Referring Party, acceptance may be effected by service of the Referral. In the case of the Responding Party, acceptance may be effected by participation in the process without objection. In some circumstances the parties (or the adjudicator) may require a formal agreement to be circulated and signed by the parties.

---

2 [2015] EWHC 661 (TCC).

The third type of appointment we see is where the adjudicator is named in the underlying contract between the parties. It is again perhaps surprising that our experience is that sometimes the first time we are aware of being named in a contract is when we are notified after a dispute has arisen (typically as an enquiry as to whether we are available to act). In other instances we will be aware as a result of an enquiry as to whether we are willing to be named or included in a list or contract. In the case of a standing DAB or DAAB, the adjudicator will typically have been required to enter into an agreement in advance. Being named in a contract can also lead to issues regarding availability and conflicts. For example, some contracts – such as maintenance contracts – have terms of many years that assume that the adjudicator will still be available to act when a dispute is referred. Further, repeat or multiple appointments from the same party can create issues regarding a perception of bias on the part of the adjudicator as a result of the volume of work or number of appointments received from one party. This can be especially so if an individual is named in a main contractor's subcontracts. We would make the point that just because an individual has been named and/or agreed by the parties to a contract to act as adjudicator does not mean that they should so act.

AVAILABILITY

One of the key considerations in deciding whether to accept an appointment is whether the prospective adjudicator has the availability to act. This is not always a straightforward consideration, not least because it is not always possible to determine how much involvement is required and/or how long the adjudication is likely to take. In some instances it might be possible to conduct an adjudication within the minimum period prescribed. In such circumstances it might be possible to predict how much time needs to be set aside, and when it is likely to be required to address initial procedural matters, review submissions and to reach and produce a Decision. However, some disputes may not readily lend themselves for determination in the minimum period prescribed. This could be on account of the complexity of the matter referred or the volume of submissions and evidence. Similarly, there may be jurisdictional challenges to address, or there might be requests for extensions of time as a result of the availability of key individuals that result in the timetable being extended or prolonged. Although it may be possible to enquire of the parties in advance of accepting an appointment as to how long the adjudication may take (e.g. when an initial enquiry is made directly by a party), this is not always possible, especially if the enquiry is from an ANA/ANB. Thus, in many instances the question of availability will be based on assumptions made as a result of considering the papers that may or may not have been provided as part of the enquiry. As a consequence, it might be sensible to qualify any willingness to act based on those assumptions and/or to disclose any future commitments or planned absences.

EXAMPLE 2.1: EMAIL CONCERNING AVAILABILITY FOLLOWING A DIRECT APPROACH FROM A PARTY'S REPRESENTATIVE TO ACT AS ADJUDICATOR

Dear [*insert name*],
Thank you for your email enquiring as to my availability to act as adjudicator in the above matter.

While I confirm that I am not aware of any matters that could constitute a conflict of interest and that I would be willing and able to accept the appointment, unfortunately I would not be able to start writing my Decision until around [*insert date*] due to my current workload. The parties would therefore need to agree an extension to the date for my Decision at the outset of the proceedings in order to accommodate my availability, most likely to be around [*insert date*], albeit this would depend on the complexity of the dispute.

I will await confirmation as to whether the parties wish to appoint me on this basis, but I entirely understand that they may wish to appoint an alternative adjudicator with more immediate availability.

Yours sincerely,

...

Notwithstanding the difficulties associated with assessing the likely amount of time involvement, an adjudicator will nevertheless have to make just such an assessment. In broad terms, there is likely to be an initial involvement in order to attend to or review the papers that have been served (e.g. the Notice of Adjudication or application form) and to attend to procedural directions. Thereafter, it may be necessary to address any objections to the appointment, which may require a more detailed review of the papers and involve considering competing submissions in a short period of time in order to decide whether the objection has any merit. Assuming that the adjudication proceeds, then time will need to be spent processing and reviewing the submissions and documents when they are served. There may also be a necessity to raise queries or meet with the parties or to visit site. Most importantly, time will need to be set aside for reaching and producing a Decision (almost invariably with reasons), and this will require reading, thinking and drafting time. Although some drafting might be possible in the earlier stages of the adjudication process, until all the submissions and documents have been provided it will not be possible to produce the substantive parts of a Decision. Finally, even after the Decision has been published, it may be necessary to attend to any corrections highlighted by the parties.

Another difficulty of assessing availability is that the start time for the adjudication timetable may not be known. This is because the time for 'referring' the dispute may be fluid. Although some legislation prescribes a period for referring a dispute after a Notice of Adjudication is given, some parties may be able to refer disputes early. For example, the UK Construction Act prescribes a period of no more than seven days from service of a Notice of Adjudication on the other side, but this does not preclude a party from referring earlier than that provided a Notice of Adjudication had been served and it was possible to do so. In contrast, in Ireland, the time period for appointment of an adjudicator by the chair of the Minister's panel is not prescribed.

A further difficulty associated with assessing availability is knowing when submissions will be made. Although some legislation and contracts may prescribe time periods for responsive submissions, not all do, and this means that both the timetable and the procedure to be adopted are left to the adjudicator's discretion. Again, assumptions will need to be made about when submissions are likely to be received and also about the number of rounds of submissions.

Once an assessment of the time involvement (and the likely dates when time is needed) is made, it will be necessary for the prospective adjudicator to consider whether they have the necessary amount of time available to devote to the task such that they are able to accept the appointment. This will require them to have good time-management skills and a good grasp of their diary commitments during the relevant period. In view of the possibility of corrections being required and the potential for a timetable to be extended, the relevant period for consideration may actually extend beyond the predicted date for a Decision.

One factor to consider is any planned absences from work, e.g. on account of parental leave or holidays. Historically, practical issues, such as availability to receive delivery of hard copies of documents, would have perhaps been a relevant factor for sole practitioners working from home or from a one-person office if they were planning on being away during the currency of an adjudication. However, in the present era of electronic communications, perhaps the key consideration is whether they will have a secure and adequate connection or access to the internet. Assuming that access to the internet and the ability to receive electronic documents and communicate electronically is not an issue, the question is then one of whether the prospective adjudicator wishes to work during such a planned absence from the office. This will ultimately be a lifestyle choice and may require consultation with those who will be affected by the election to work while on planned leave. However, even then, the possibility of a meeting or site inspection may mean that absence from the office is an issue, especially if the adjudicator is abroad and operating in an incompatible or challenging time zone.

In our view, providing that a planned absence does not affect an adjudicator's ability to manage the process, to consider the submissions and evidence, and to reach and produce a Decision within either a prescribed or agreed timetable, then it should not in itself prevent an adjudicator accepting an appointment. The corollary of this is that if it does, or is considered likely to, affect the ability to manage the process, then it would be inappropriate to accept an invitation to act.

One further point to note is that, in our experience, parties who have agreed that an adjudicator should act may be more likely to accommodate planned absences, future work commitments or holidays. This is especially the case if the timetable is likely to be extended in any event or where time is not so pressing, e.g. when the project is historic or when the parties have already spent significant time preparing for an adjudication. This is not to say that it would not be possible for an adjudicator to inform an ANA/ANB of planned absence, but it may be impractical for the ANA/ANB to engage or liaise with either one or both parties to see whether they are willing to accommodate a planned absence. This is particularly so where an ANA/ANB is under a strict timetable to appoint.

CONFLICTS

In our view, the question of whether an adjudicator may have a conflict of interest is the most important consideration when deciding whether to accept an appointment. This is because, in the event that an adjudicator is found to have a conflict of interest, it is very likely that any Decision they reach will be rendered unenforceable or a nullity. This is on account of the Decision being obtained as a result of a serious breach of the rules of natural justice and, specifically, the requirement that the adjudicator is to be impartial and independent of the parties. It is therefore imperative that a prospective adjudicator has a sound understanding of the applicable principles, the ability to understand whether a past or present involvement may give rise to a conflict, and also the ability to be able to conduct an enquiry in a relatively short period of time.

The concept of conflicts of interest concerns the question of whether a set of circumstances or an involvement would give rise to a perception that an adjudicator would be biased towards or against a party on account of such circumstances or involvement. In the United Kingdom the relevant test is not whether there is actual bias, but whether bias would be perceived. The test is considered objectively from the view of the informed observer. Although the question of whether a set of circumstances or an involvement gives rise to a conflict of interest is to be assessed objectively and from the view of the informed observer, it is the adjudicator who will need to conduct that initial assessment in order to form a view as to whether they are able to accept an appointment in the first place.

Thankfully, there is some guidance available to dispute resolvers. Although some of the guidance is aimed at arbitrators, the principles are the same. Thus, the International Bar Association (IBA) publish the 'IBA Guidelines on Conflicts of Interest in International Arbitration' (hereafter referred to as the IBA Guidelines).[3] Similarly, the Royal Institution of Chartered Surveyors (RICS) publish a guidance note titled 'Conflicts

3 International Bar Association. 2024. IBA Guidelines on Conflicts of Interest in International Arbitration (https://bit.ly/3wFOCTt).

of interest for members acting as dispute resolvers' that is intended to encompass any third-party neutral appointment and specifically covers adjudicators.[4] Helpfully, both the IBA Guidelines and the RICS guidance note provide examples of situations and involvements that may give rise to a conflict and examples of those that do not. They also both adopt a traffic light type system, with involvements categorised as red, amber/orange or green, with examples in the red list representing a conflict, examples in the amber/orange list giving rise to an obligation to make a disclosure and/or obtain consent, and examples in the green list not constituting a conflict or requiring any disclosure. It should be noted, however, that the examples are not exhaustive, and what is considered to be a conflict may alter over time.

Situations that represent obvious examples of conflicts would be where the adjudicator is employed by, or has a significant shareholding in, one of the parties, or where the party is a close family member. In such circumstances it is clear how there could be a perception that the adjudicator would be predisposed towards and/or have an interest in that party doing well. At the other end of the spectrum, the fact that a person has previously acted as an adjudicator in an unrelated matter involving one of the parties could not be said to give rise to an obvious conflict of interest. However, what if the person had received multiple appointments from one party and, as a result, derived significant income from those appointments? Depending on the facts, it might be appropriate to disclose such previous appointments (while being mindful not to breach any confidentiality) or to decline an appointment.

RELEVANT CASE LAW

While it is a case concerning an arbitrator, rather than an adjudicator, reference should be made to the UK Commercial Court case of *Cofely Limited v Anthony Bingham and Knowles Limited*[5] where the arbitrator was removed due to the risk of apparent bias. This in part arose from concerns over his relationship with the representative of one of the parties to the arbitration.

---

4 RICS. 2020. Conflicts of interest for members acting as dispute resolvers, 2nd edition. Guidance note, November (https://bit.ly/44UlVPo).

5 [2016] EWHC 240 (Comm).

It is not only the relationship with the parties that is relevant, but also the relationship with the parties' representatives and advisors. In a specialist industry or market it may be that the community is relatively small, such that the adjudicator is known to the representatives (and vice versa). Perhaps he or she might have been involved on unrelated matters, or met them through professional or industry organizations or committees, or shared with them platforms at conferences, etc. In itself this may not be an issue, especially if these involvements are common between both sets of party representatives or are in the public domain. However, if there is an imbalance and/or the adjudicator is, for example, regularly instructed and/or is working as an expert with one of the party's advisors, this might lead to a perceived conflict. It is therefore important to consider each set of circumstances and to continually review whether a situation is such to give rise to a perception of bias.

On a practical note, it is also important to have a system in place to enable a conflict of interest check to be made. Although it is possible for an adjudicator to remember the historic involvements they might have, the human memory is not infallible. We therefore recommend that a record or database is kept of past and current appointments so that a check can be undertaken. This could be as simple as conducting a name search in an electronic archive: this might be sufficient if the prospective adjudicator is either a sole practitioner or works in a small practice with shared electronic storage systems. However, in a larger organization with multiple offices across different countries, a more sophisticated system might be required. Indeed, if the prospective adjudicator is employed by a large multinational law or expert firm, they might well have a 'conflict check' system or department devoted to this task. In short, the point is that everyone wanting to act as an adjudicator should have a system in place.

Another point we would make is that, even if the prospective adjudicator does not consider an involvement or set of circumstances to give rise to a conflict, it may still be advisable not to accept an appointment. This may be because that involvement may make things uncomfortable for them or give rise to a future conflict or difficult situation. For example, the prospective adjudicator may know that it is likely that they will come across someone in the future at an event that could put them in a difficult situation on account of finding against the party they are employed by and/or represent. If this is not a situation the prospective adjudicator is comfortable with, they may elect not to accept an appointment notwithstanding the fact that there is no current conflict perceived or otherwise.

Sometimes, the safest approach to adopt if in doubt about whether an involvement may constitute a conflict is simply to make a disclosure of that involvement. As well as being generally good practice, we would also note that an insignificant involvement that could have been disclosed at the outset of the proceedings may well be perceived very differently if it is discovered by a disgruntled losing party after the adjudicator's Decision has been published. Furthermore, while we are concerned here with the pre-appointment stage, it should also be remembered that the duty of impartiality is a continuing one, such that it may be necessary to review and/or make disclosures as a result of circumstances that come to light after an appointment has been made: for example, where a party's representative or expert is unknown until after the appointment or as a result of coming into contact with a party, a witness or a representative at an event during the currency of an adjudication.

SKILLS

Another consideration for the prospective adjudicator is whether they possess the necessary skills to accept the appointment. This may be relevant if the underlying contract or enquiry prescribes a particular skill or qualification, i.e. an essential requirement, or if there is a professional obligation or implied term that the adjudicator should be competent to undertake the role, or merely if there is a skill that one or both of the parties would like the adjudicator to possess.

To the extent the contract stipulates a required qualification, the question will be binary: the adjudicator will either possess the qualification or will not. Sometimes a contract will prescribe that the adjudicator shall possess a qualification or have held such a qualification for a period of time, or that the adjudicator must be included on a published list. We are also aware of some contracts that seek to prescribe different qualifications for different types of dispute. For example, for disputes concerning valuation, a quantity surveyor should be appointed; for disputes concerning contractual interpretation, a practising lawyer should be appointed; and so on. In the context of construction contracts, where disputes may be multifaceted, this is not free from difficulty. It is not hard to envisage a situation in which a dispute over an entitlement to payment could encompass legal issues, engineering issues, architectural issues, delay-related issues, questions of whether a professional has fallen below a required standard of skill and care, and quantum issues.

Assuming that the contract does not prescribe a qualification, then it may be that a party making an enquiry or an application to an ANA/ANB nevertheless requests that the adjudicator possesses a qualification or skillset or has experience or knowledge of a certain type of contract. In such circumstances it is important that the prospective adjudicator makes clear whether they satisfy the request and/or provides clarification as to their qualifications or experience. Once such clarification is made, the party or ANA/ANB can elect to proceed with the appointment in that knowledge, or can decide not to do so. It may also be a requirement of the ANA/ANB that the prospective adjudicator confirms whether or not they comply with any requirements included in the application. It is therefore important not to misrepresent the position as doing so may invalidate the appointment.

The types of dispute that typically arise under or in connection with construction contracts will usually concern issues associated with time, money or quality. As well as factual issues, there might be

- legal issues that require an understanding of the law and contractual interpretation,
- technical issues that require an ability to understand engineering or architectural matters,
- contested entitlements to extensions of time or liquidated damages that require an understanding of how delay analysis is conducted and which methodology is appropriate under a contract, and
- quantum issues that require an understanding of the applicable valuation rules or causation.

In our view it is unlikely that any one individual can be said to be an expert in every possible facet of a construction project. However, it needs to be remembered that (thankfully!) the role of the adjudicator is not to act as an expert in the same way that may be required when providing expert evidence in the context of litigation or arbitration proceedings.

Our view is that the role of an adjudicator is quasi-judicial. Although the approach of a judge may vary between common law and civil law jurisdictions, ultimately nothing turns on this in respect of adjudication. This is because, irrespective of which jurisdiction an adjudicator is acting in – and notwithstanding the fact they will inevitably possess inquisitorial powers – they are obliged to reach a Decision in a procedurally fair manner. In order to do so they will be required to take into account the parties' submissions and the evidence provided. In the event they wish to reach a Decision based on matters that have not been advanced by the parties (e.g. as a result of their expertise), they will be obliged to invite comment during the adjudication proceedings: to do otherwise could render their Decision unenforceable. In reaching a Decision, an adjudicator will also need to take into account which party has the burden of proof in respect of each contested issue, and they will need to reach a Decision based on whether the relevant party has satisfied the standard of proof required. It is therefore for the parties to make out their respective cases and for the adjudicator to reach a Decision based on the parties' submissions and the evidence provided.

As a consequence of the multifaceted nature of the types of dispute that may arise under or in connection with construction contracts and because of the quasi-judicial nature of the adjudication process, our view is that an adjudicator needs to have an understanding of the applicable legal principles and the underlying contract and be able to understand the submissions and evidence that are being presented. This should not require the adjudicator to be an expert in a particular area, but the adjudicator does need to have the ability to read and understand a technical drawing, to understand principles and methods of construction, to understand a delay analysis, to be able to navigate a spreadsheet, to understand how a contract should be administered, and so on. An adjudicator may also be required to consider legal authorities and apply the relevant law to the applicable facts. In our view these skills are likely to be acquired as a combination of vocational education, experience and specific training in how to manage an adjudication and to reach and write a reasoned Decision.

THE APPROACH OF DIFFERENT NOMINATING BODIES AND APPOINTING AUTHORITIES

The approach adopted by ANAs/ANBs to appointment varies. However, our experience is that there are two main differences in respect of how they either draw up a list or select individuals. The first relates to how the shortlist or initial selection is made at the initial enquiry stage. The second relates to whether the enquiry is sent to one or more prospective adjudicators. Although there are other variations, our view is that these are more administrative in nature (e.g. whether enquiries are made by telephone or email).

In relation to how the shortlist or initial selection is made, the main difference is whether there is an exercise of discretion or whether a 'cab rank' approach is adopted. Where discretion is to be exercised, the authority is likely to take into account the application received and any specific requests and will then select either one or a number of potentially suitable candidates to act. Once that process has been completed, an enquiry will be sent to the candidate(s) identified asking them to confirm whether they are aware of any conflicts of interest and, if not, whether they are available to act if selected. As part of the enquiry process the prospective adjudicator(s) will be asked to consider the papers (typically, but not always, a copy of the Notice of Adjudication, the application form and any other relevant documentation or correspondence) and then to confirm whether they are willing and able to act if selected. The response to the enquiry is typically required in relatively short order and may also require undertakings to be made regarding compliance with any criteria set down by the nominating authority. These undertakings may include confirmation that the prospective adjudicator has the required level of expertise, is available, complies with any special requirements and has appropriate insurance cover. They may also require the prospective adjudicator to confirm that they comply with conditions imposed by the nominating authority, e.g. keeping up to date with CPD, subjecting themself to any complaints-handling process, and, importantly, confirming there is no conflict of interest (which may be in the form of a declaration of impartiality and independence). Once confirmation is given, the nominating authority will progress to the next stage, i.e. the appointment or nomination.

Instead of adopting a discretionary selection process, some nominating authorities will adopt a cab rank approach, whereby they will work through the list in a specific order. Although there may also be an element of adjustment required (e.g. if the application or underlying contract requires a specific qualification), the basic principle with the cab rank approach is that anyone who has satisfied the criteria for inclusion on the list or roster is capable of acting as an adjudicator and selection will therefore be based on a sequential selection process. Once a candidate has been selected, they will then move to the bottom of the list and progress to the top of the list as and when others have been selected, i.e. the candidate will normally have to wait until others on the list or roster have received an appointment before they are selected again. We understand that some nominating authorities will adjust their procedure in certain circumstances, e.g. if there is a series of adjudications between the same parties under one contract and it appears sensible for the same adjudicator to act. Once an adjudicator is identified (based on being at the top of the list), they will be sent an enquiry in the same way as a candidate under the 'discretionary' system.

The next difference adopted is whether the enquiry is sent to one or more candidates. From our perspective, if the prospective adjudicator knows they are the only candidate being approached, it is easier to commit and plan on the basis that, assuming they satisfy all the criteria and are willing and able to act, the chances that they will be selected are reasonably high. In contrast, if the prospective adjudicator is on a list of potential candidates, they may have to wait a short while for confirmation as to whether they have been appointed. From a practical perspective, in the former situation the prospective adjudicator may be able to proceed with preparing their initial communication and directions, whereas it may be unwise to do so in the latter situation on the basis that they may not be appointed. From the nominating authority's perspective, we can understand that only going to one candidate may reduce the administrative workload, although in the event a sole candidate is not available it may lengthen the appointment process. For this reason, we are aware that some nominating authorities may make a preliminary enquiry before sending the full documentation to see whether a candidate is available to act in principle in order to avoid delay.

Once a candidate has confirmed both their availability and their willingness to act, the nominating body or authority will need to select the adjudicator and confirm the nomination or appointment to the parties and the adjudicator. It is not until confirmation of the nomination or appointment that the adjudicator is in post. From a contractual perspective, it may be that the nomination concludes the contract between the parties and the adjudicator. If this is the case, then a question arises as to whether an adjudicator can impose or incorporate their terms into that contract. Our view is that, to the extent the terms are not already prescribed or set by the nominating authority or legislation, an adjudicator will need to obtain agreement or acceptance of their terms following nomination by the nominating authority. We address terms in the next section.

Finally, on this topic, from a practical perspective – in view of the fast-track nature and the shortage of time available for the nominating authority to appoint an adjudicator – potential candidates will need to ensure that they are available to respond quickly to any enquiry. As well as considering the documentation provided, this may involve undertaking a conflict check and completing and returning any declaration required by the nominating authority. Our experience is that enquiries are not necessarily restricted to typical 'office hours', and responses may be required during the evenings and at weekends in order to comply with any deadlines imposed by the nominating authority or the applicable legislation. We are certainly aware of nominating authorities having to go elsewhere on account of a lack of a response from a prospective adjudicator. The other thing to note is that it may also be helpful for adjudicators to advise the nominating authority if they are likely to be unavailable for a period of time on account of other commitments.

TERMS

We have already alluded to the contractual position and to the potential difference between a nomination or appointment by a nominating authority on the one hand and a direct appointment on the other. However, irrespective of the type of appointment, it is important to establish the applicable terms.

In certain jurisdictions, terms (including fees) may be prescribed by the primary or secondary legislation, and therefore a nominating authority may have the power to impose the terms and/or fees that apply. In such circumstances an adjudicator will be obliged to work to those terms, which may well be a condition of their appointment or inclusion on a panel.

Similarly, the terms and fees may be prescribed by the underlying contract or procedural rules either in whole or in part. For example, certain procedural rules may impose a fixed fee based on the amount in dispute. Other rules may impose a maximum hourly rate combined with a cap on the overall fee. Others may prescribe terms but leave the hourly rate to be inserted by the adjudicator and agreed by the parties. For example, both the NEC and FIDIC allow an adjudicator to insert a daily rate, and FIDIC also provides for a retainer based on an assumed level of involvement. If the contract prescribes the use of particular terms such as the NEC4 Dispute Resolution Service Contract, but the parties make no mention of this, we would recommend that the adjudicator checks with the parties as to whether they wish these terms to apply.

Assuming that an adjudicator has the freedom or ability to agree terms, then they will need to have a set available for distribution and/or agreement. The most common terms provide for payment based on the time spent on the matter at an hourly rate and allow for recovery of expenses at cost. Some terms will differentiate between travel time and time spent working on the matter, and they might also include for subsistence in the event of overnight trips spent away from home.

The extent to which an adjudicator is able to impose a lien or require payment in advance of releasing their Decision will depend on the governing legislation case law and/or the applicable adjudication rules. In the United Kingdom, for example, the courts will not allow an adjudicator to impose a lien, although it is thought that it may be possible for a lien to be imposed if the parties expressly agree to it. To overcome the issue, we are aware that some adjudicators in the United Kingdom will provide for an appointment fee or interim payments on account in advance of reaching their Decision, although they may not be able to delay or defer publication of their Decision in the event a party does not pay. This arrangement can lead to difficulties if one party has paid and another has not, and/or it can give rise to allegations of bias if an adjudicator requires payment from only one party.

Assuming that a lien and/or advance payment cannot be imposed or agreed, an adjudicator may wish to prescribe a period for payment and also provide for interest in the event of late payment. We are also aware that some adjudicators include a term that enables them to charge for any time spent chasing or pursuing their fees. This is perhaps understandable for sole practitioners, who may otherwise have to turn down work on account of having to pursue bad debts.

Another provision commonly included in an adjudicator's terms is an immunity from suit, save for instances of bad faith. Although most legislation and contracts typically provide for such immunity, this is not always the position, so an adjudicator would be well advised to include such provisions.

Finally, we are aware that some adjudicators include a provision that they are entitled to be paid irrespective of whether or not their Decision is enforceable. Again, this is perhaps understandable, especially if the reason for a Decision not being enforced is not attributable to any wrongful conduct on the part of the adjudicator, e.g. where there was some procedural irregularity in the appointment process that only came to light after the Decision had been reached. However, we are also aware that some parties and representatives consider such terms to be unreasonable because they may result in an adjudicator being entitled to payment even in circumstances where their own actions or inactions result in an unenforceable Decision. If objections are raised to such terms, it will be a commercial decision for the adjudicator as to whether they wish to proceed with the adjudication.

INITIAL DIRECTIONS

Irrespective of whether the appointment is a result of a nomination, agreement by the parties or being named in a contract, the first thing for the adjudicator to do upon appointment is to confirm their appointment and provide their initial directions.

Ordinarily, the adjudicator will have been given contact details for both parties: typically email and postal addresses. However, this is not always the position: sometimes an adjudicator is nominated without the applicant having included an email address or confirmation of who is representing the Responding Party. In such circumstances, it may be that contact details need to be obtained from the Referring Party or otherwise. Ideally, obtaining details and any unilateral contact should be undertaken by another member of the adjudicator's firm. However, if the adjudicator is a sole practitioner, there may not be an individual to delegate this task to. If that is the case, then, in the interests of transparency, a record of any unilateral communication should be kept. Once contact details have been obtained, communications can proceed, making sure that both parties are copied in. If communications are electronic, it may be prudent to set up delivery and/or read receipts as a means of monitoring whether emails are delivered and/or read. This can be particularly helpful when faced with a recalcitrant party or a reluctant participant to the proceedings in order for the adjudicator to satisfy themself (or a third party, such as a judge, if necessary) that communications have been delivered. If there is still uncertainty as to whether a party is receiving emails, we would also suggest sending hard copy correspondence by a means that can be tracked and for which proof of delivery is obtained, e.g. signed-for tracked post.

To the extent it is permissible, and on the assumption that agreement to our terms has not already been obtained (e.g. as a result of a direct appointment), our practice is to confirm that acceptance of an appointment or nomination is subject to our terms and also the applicable adjudication provisions. Although our approach is not to obtain express agreement to our terms, we appreciate that some adjudicators seek to obtain such agreement. Our rationale for not doing so is that it may actually result in agreement being held not to have been given on account of a lack of express confirmation. Conversely, acceptance of terms may be deemed to be inferred or there may be acceptance by conduct. However, we acknowledge that where an adjudicator is nominated it is arguable that, as a contract was concluded upon nomination, it is not permissible to unilaterally impose terms. In such circumstances, it may be that an adjudicator is entitled to a reasonable fee. In determining what represents a reasonable fee, our view is that the normal terms or rates that are levied by an adjudicator may well be a relevant consideration.

As well as confirming acceptance of the appointment and notifying fees, it is important to provide directions regarding the conduct of the adjudication. Things that will typically need to be covered will be directions about how an adjudicator wishes to receive communications such as procedural correspondence and submissions. Although experienced representatives will understand the convention that all communications with the adjudicator should be copied to the other side at the same time and by the same means, this may not be the case with inexperienced representatives or unrepresented parties. In a similar vein, it may be necessary to give directions either to discourage contact by telephone or to direct that the adjudicator is not to be contacted by telephone. This is to avoid any issue arising from unilateral communications. However, there may be exceptions to this, e.g. to advise of an administrative issue (such as an internet or network failure). The point here is that directions for ground rules may need to be given as the parties may not be aware of the conventions adopted for conducting adjudication proceedings.

Our current practice is for all communications and submissions to only be provided electronically. However, we are aware that some adjudicators still prefer to receive documents in hard copy. Given the electronic file size of certain documents (e.g. drawings, photographs or videos), it may be sensible to prescribe attachment size limits to account for any inbox limits and/or to direct that large documents are provided via a file transfer portal or via download links. It may also be sensible to give directions regarding the following.

- The length of file and folder names for electronic files: our experience is that sometimes excessive lengths can cause issues with access, especially where files have been compressed.

- The format of the documents, e.g. for them to be in a searchable format such as a searchable PDF or Word document. We find the ability to search for words in electronic documents invaluable during the adjudication process. It may also be sensible to direct the parties to provide programmes, spreadsheets, etc., in their native electronic format; this pre-empts the inevitable request from the other party for native documents.

Although it is not our practice, we are aware of one adjudicator who prescribes how witness statements or expert reports are to be presented. Although we see no reason for this (the parties are free to present evidence in such manner as they see fit), the key point is that if you as an adjudicator wish for communications, submissions or evidence to be presented in a certain format, this needs to be directed.

Although a Referring Party should be aware of any time limit for service of the Referral, they might not be. For this reason we advocate recording when we expect or require the Referral to be served, taking into account any time limit that is prescribed by the applicable legislation or contract. Alternatively, it may be that there is no time limit prescribed, e.g. in the case of an ad hoc DAB appointment, such that it may actually be appropriate to convene a preliminary meeting with the parties in order to agree a date for service of the Referral.

Additionally, it may be advisable to give directions as to any mandatory elements to be included with the Referral submissions. For example, the contract or applicable legislation may require a copy or relevant extracts of the contract to be provided, or it might stipulate that the Referral needs to set out the specific redress or relief sought. Although it sounds obvious, confirmation that the Referral is to be accompanied by all documents and evidence relied upon may also be something an adjudicator wishes to direct.

Finally, although we are aware that some adjudicators will issue directions for the overall timetable to be adopted at this stage, in our view the overall timetable and the procedure to be adopted are topics best addressed once the content and extent of the Referral are known. There are two main reasons we adopt this approach. First, the date of the Referral may be unknown, e.g. it may be served before the deadline. Second, and this is perhaps more important, until the Referral is served it may not be possible to realistically assess what timetable or procedure is appropriate to adopt. Although a Notice of Adjudication should provide some details of the dispute, this is unlikely to be extensive. In contrast, a Referral should set out in full the submissions supporting the Referring Party's contentions and should be accompanied by supporting evidence. Consequently, our approach is to record in our initial directions that we will address the timetable and procedure to be adopted following service of the Referral.

EXAMPLE 2.2: EXAMPLE INITIAL DIRECTIONS

Dear [*insert names*],
As the parties may have been advised, I have been nominated by [*insert nominating body*] to act as adjudicator in a dispute between [*insert Referring Party's name*] and [*insert Responding Party's name*]. I have not seen a copy of the contract between the parties and I therefore accept the nomination on the basis of the applicable adjudication provisions and the attached Terms of Appointment.

The parties should note that every communication to me should bear on its face confirmation that it has been copied to the other side at the same time and by the same means. All correspondence from me will be directed to the parties or their representatives where appointed. I would prefer

- all procedural correspondence and submissions to be made electronically by email or uploaded to a file hosting service (please note that the path lengths of files and folders should not exceed a total of 250 characters in order to avoid problems in saving and opening downloaded files);

- the written narratives in the submissions, including witness statements and expert reports, to (i) be in a searchable format, e.g. searchable PDF or Word; (ii) state the page number and document title on every page, either in the header or footer; and (iii) include a contents page (or contents pages) for all appendices/exhibits where appropriate;

- programmes, spreadsheets, etc., to be provided in their original electronic format where possible.

I ask that email 'read receipts' are provided when requested. Communication by telephone should be restricted to urgent administrative matters only.

The Referring Party should now proceed to issue the Referral. The Referral should be accompanied by copies of, or relevant extracts from, the contract and from such other documents as the Referring Party intends to rely upon. Upon receipt of the Referral I shall invite the parties to agree a mutually convenient timetable for the adjudication. I note that the Notice of Adjudication is dated [*insert date of the notice*] and the Referral should therefore be served on or before [*insert date on which Referral should be served*].

Yours sincerely,

. . .

DEALING WITH OBJECTIONS TO APPOINTMENT

In our experience it is not unknown for the Responding Party to object to the appointment of an adjudicator. Although we set out how to address challenges to jurisdiction in chapter 4, we consider that early objections to an appointment warrant a separate (albeit brief) mention, especially if they precede service of the Referral itself.

We are aware that one school of thought is that the appointment is not effected until the Referral is served. We do not share this view. Although service of the Referral may trigger the timetable and the obligation to reach a Decision, we consider that the appointment of the adjudicator commences when either a nomination is made or when acceptance of an appointment is confirmed. Nevertheless, as the obligation to proceed to reach a Decision is dependent on a Referral being served, it may be prudent to defer consideration of any challenge to an appointment until after service of the Referral. This is because the Referring Party may elect not to proceed in light of the objection, thereby avoiding the adjudicator spending any time addressing the objection unnecessarily.

If an objection is received prior to service of the Referral, the approach that we adopt will depend on whether it is possible to discern immediately whether the objection has merit. If it appears to have merit, it may be possible to address it in relatively short order and avoid the need for the Referral to be served and/or enable any defect in the appointment to be rectified. Conversely, where it is not readily apparent whether the challenge has merit, it may be sensible to ask the Referring Party to address the challenge no later than the date it serves the Referral. This will then enable the challenge to be investigated as soon as the Referral is served.

CHAPTER 3

Initial procedural considerations

In this chapter we focus on matters that an adjudicator might have to take into account or manage when deciding on what timetable to adopt. Case management, in terms of managing the procedure, is a significant part of the adjudicator's role. In some ways it can be more challenging than the decision-making function, particularly if there is a reluctant party. As well as timetabling issues, we highlight some features that may arise from concurrent or serial adjudications, as well as dealing with insolvent parties.

TIMETABLING ISSUES

As already mentioned, one of the common features of the adjudication process across jurisdictions and contracts is the requirement to reach a Decision within a prescribed period of time. Although some sets of procedural rules prescribe a timetable for the making of submissions, this is not universal – and even when a timetable is prescribed, there may be requests for additional time from the parties or circumstances that render the prescribed timetable redundant. In most circumstances an adjudicator will have the discretion and the power to set the timetable for the making of submissions and for the procedure that is to be adopted. Good case-management skills will therefore be required by the adjudicator to ensure that the adjudication is conducted in a manner that is consistent with the overriding purpose of the process.

So what is the overriding purpose of an adjudication? From the adjudicator's perspective it must be to produce a Decision in respect of the dispute that has been referred. That Decision needs to be produced within the time that has been imposed by legislation and/or the contract, and it will need to be produced in a manner that is procedurally fair. The Decision may also be required to have reasons. All of these factors are interrelated, but a key feature of adjudication is the time pressures or constraints under which the adjudicator (and the parties) operate in order to achieve the overriding purpose.

In determining the timetable and the procedure to be adopted, the question of whether the adjudicator is the 'master or mistress of the procedure' or the 'servant of the parties' can arise? To some extent the approach adopted will vary between different adjudicators. Some will adopt a 'my way or the highway' approach, while others will be more collegiate and defer to the parties, inviting them to liaise in an attempt to agree a timetable, but always subject to the adjudicator's approval. In the event that the parties are unable to agree, then the adjudicator will have to make a decision as to what constitutes a reasonable timetable, taking into account the parties' respective positions and any constraints imposed by the legislation and/or the contract in respect of the overall period.

It is fair to say that the approach we take has changed since the impact of the Covid-19 pandemic on working practice, and, in particular, the effect the pandemic had on workplace restrictions and the move towards home working. Although remote working and the use of online meeting platforms is commonplace nowadays, this was not the situation before 2020 – not in the case of dispute resolution at least. During the pandemic we were particularly conscious that people's ability to download, access and print documents might be restricted, and that the facilities available for this when working from home were unlikely to match those found in offices. Likewise, an individual's circumstances might differ – in our personal cases, the demands of homeschooling and teenagers streaming films added to the challenge! Similarly, the ability to send or receive hard copy documents was impacted, e.g. some offices were not staffed to enable deliveries to be made. We therefore tended towards a more collegiate approach whereby we would invite the parties to liaise in an attempt to reach agreement on the timetable or procedure to be adopted. Failing agreement, we directed that they revert to us with their respective positions as to an appropriate timetable. To a certain extent we had already adopted that approach in complex or large cases, but we adopted it more universally during the period where working and travel restrictions were imposed as a result of the pandemic, and we have continued to work in this way since.

In our view, the obligation to comply with the timescales prescribed by legislation and/or the contract is subordinate to the obligation to conduct an adjudication in a procedurally fair manner. Thus, if an adjudicator forms the view that it is not possible to conduct an adjudication and produce a Decision within the prescribed timetables without affording the parties a reasonable opportunity of responding to the case and evidence advanced against them, then, in the absence of agreement to extend the timetable, our view is that the correct course of action is to resign. In our experience, when we have suggested that we would resign in such circumstances, the parties have tended to reach an agreement to extend. From a practical perspective, when faced with the realization that it will take some time to appoint a new adjudicator and/or that the dispute is likely to be referred to a different adjudicator, it may be better for the parties to agree to an extended timetable. It is worth adding that the adjudicator's view as to what constitutes a reasonable timetable may carry weight in the event a party seeks to resist enforcement on account of a timetable that they contend was unfair. Again, this is another factor that might influence a party's decision to agree to an extended timetable.

Although there are a multitude of types of dispute that may arise under or in connection with a construction contract, in broad terms we consider there to be two categories of dispute that are referred to adjudication: those that can be conducted within the minimum periods prescribed by statute or contract and those that cannot. These could be referred to as 'simple' in the former case, perhaps confined to a small number of issues, and 'large' or 'complex' in the latter, e.g. a dispute concerning a final account on a large project. These types of dispute are sometimes referred to as 'kitchen sink adjudications'.

We think of 'simple' adjudications as being those that concern disputes that lend themselves to being resolved within the statutory minimum periods in which a 'documents only' procedure is adopted. An example of this might be a single-issue dispute such as a claim for a notified sum due to the lack of necessary notices. With this type of dispute it is more likely for us to set a timetable without inviting the parties to liaise. The approach we generally adopt is to work back from the date by which we are obliged to reach a Decision (typically calculated from the date the Referral is served, although in some jurisdictions time may be calculated from the date of the appointment). This will require an assessment of the time that may be required for the adjudicator to consider the submissions, reach their conclusion and draft the Decision. We tend to leave a period of one week for this purpose. This is not to say a full week will be required, but in our experience one week provides sufficient time to undertake the task, and it is a timeframe that allows us to also attend to other matters during this period. What we typically do is set a cut-off time or 'guillotine' for submissions. Although we would not necessarily disallow or disregard submissions that arrive after the cut off, we might warn the parties that we may not be able to take full account of late submissions unless an extension of time is agreed to facilitate doing so. So, assuming a 28-day procedure, that leaves 21 days for submissions. We will typically allow seven to ten days for a Response and between five and seven days for a Reply, with the balance of the period (seven days, say) allowed for further submissions subject to prior permission being sought and consent being granted. We address how such requests can be dealt with both later in this chapter and in chapter 5.

EXAMPLE 3.1: EXAMPLE DIRECTIONS TEMPLATE IN A 'SIMPLE' CASE

Dear [*insert names*],
I acknowledge receipt of the Referral by email timed at [*insert time*] today. Accordingly, [*insert reference to public holidays which need to be taken into account*] I am obliged to reach my Decision on or before [*insert date*]. My directions for the procedure to be adopted in this adjudication are therefore as follows.

- The Responding Party is to submit its Response, which should include a written statement of the contentions on which it relies and any material it wishes me to consider, by [*insert time if appropriate, and date*].

- The Referring Party may submit a Reply to the Response by [*insert time if appropriate, and date*].

- Any submissions beyond the Reply, either in response to an invitation by me or at the request of either party with my permission, to be made no later than [*insert date*]. While I would not necessarily deny either party the opportunity to make submissions after this date, I must warn the parties that I may not be able to give them full consideration in reaching my Decision by [*insert date*].

I now look forward to receiving the Response on or before [*insert time if appropriate, and date*].

Yours sincerely,

...

Turning to 'large' or 'complex' adjudications, i.e. those concerning disputes that do not lend themselves to being decided in the statutory minimum period or without the need for a meeting, we are more likely to engage with the parties regarding an appropriate timetable. So, as already alluded to, upon receipt of the Referral we would invite the parties to liaise in an attempt to agree a timetable and a procedure. Depending on the experience of the representatives, we may provide a structure (with dates to be filled in) or give the parties free rein to agree and propose a timetable for our approval. We might also prescribe a period for us to reach our Decision, although assessing the period of time that may be required can be more difficult in these types of cases, such that we may seek to caveat any approval of a timetable as being subject to review once all submissions have been served.

EXAMPLE 3.2: EXAMPLE TEMPLATE EMAIL INVITING THE PARTIES TO AGREE THE ADJUDICATION TIMETABLE

Dear [*insert names*],

I acknowledge receipt of the Referral by email timed at [*insert time*] today, including a [*insert name of computer file transfer service*] link to the appendices. I confirm that I have been able to download the appendices.

I now ask the parties to

- liaise and attempt to agree a mutually convenient timetable for the adjudication; for the avoidance of doubt, I do *not* need to be copied in on the parties' discussions concerning the timetable;

- advise me by [*insert time and date*] whether they have been able to agree a mutually convenient timetable and, if so, confirm what that timetable is; if the parties are unable to agree a mutually convenient timetable, then I ask each party to set out what it considers a fair timetable to be in the circumstances; I will thereafter set out what I consider a fair timetable to be.

Yours sincerely,

...

In an ideal world, the parties would agree a timetable and, subject to it working for the adjudicator, formal adoption of the timetable can then be confirmed and directed. However, agreement is not always possible, especially when the parties and their representatives are at loggerheads and (perhaps) seeking to gain a tactical advantage over the opposing side. This then requires an assessment of what constitutes a procedurally fair timetable. As already mentioned, the obligation to comply with a statutory or contractual timetable is, in our view, subordinate to the obligation to comply with the rules of natural justice. Thus, if the adjudicator forms the view that it is not possible to deliver a Decision that enables them to comply with their obligations in respect of natural justice, the appropriate course of action is to stand down. In deciding what constitutes a procedurally fair timetable, relevant factors might include the extent to which the arguments, information or evidence provided are new; the volume of the material provided; the complexity of the subject matter; the amount in dispute; the significance of the impact of the claim; and the need for urgency.

Although some argue that it is not permissible to advance new arguments or provide previously unseen evidence, the tendency is for adjudicators to allow such submissions and materials provided they fall within the ambit of the dispute that has been referred; it would also be subject to the proviso that the other side has a reasonable opportunity to consider it and respond. This will be very much fact dependent, but things to consider will be the availability of key individuals or the extent to which outside expert resource is required. In our experience timetables of between two and three months are not untypical. Interestingly, that period falls within both the 84-day timetable prescribed by the FIDIC conditions and the 100-day timetable that was advocated by the Society of Construction Arbitrators when looking to introduce a 'fast-track' arbitration procedure for construction industry disputes. Some might say that construction adjudication has now actually developed into a fast-track arbitration procedure, with the only material difference being its temporarily binding effect and the absence of the powers to award party costs.

Another feature of larger or more complex disputes is the fact that a meeting or hearing might be required. We address the factors to consider in deciding whether to hold a meeting and how to prepare and conduct such a meeting in chapter 6, and, for present purposes, we consider only the timetabling considerations here. In our view, if there is a likelihood that a meeting will be required, then it is desirable to set a date in advance so that any decision to hold such a meeting does not cause any delay to the timetable at a later date. We would typically aim to set a meeting date after the final timetabled submission but before the cut off for any final submissions. If the last submission set down in the adjudication timetable is the Reply, we would normally seek to schedule the meeting date a few days afterwards so that the content of the Reply could be considered and taken into account prior to the meeting. The reason for setting the meeting prior to the cut-off date for any further submissions is to allow for any matters or actions arising from the meeting to be factored into the timetable. Sometimes it may not be possible to agree a 'provisional' meeting date, e.g. where potential attendees are unavailable, and there can become a point where it may be better to defer setting or addressing the meeting date until after a firm decision is made as to whether a meeting is required. Time might otherwise be wasted trying to agree a provisional date for a meeting and/or an unduly lengthy adjudication timetable may result from having to accommodate everyone's availability, which will be particularly frustrating if it turns out that a meeting is not required.

The same issues that fall to be considered when setting a meeting date also arise in the context of setting a date for a site inspection. Again, we address both the factors to consider in deciding whether to hold a site inspection and other logistical issues in chapter 6, but an added complication when setting down a site inspection date is that access may not be within the control of the parties, e.g. access to a rail project or a military or government property might require specific consents or an induction by a third party, or the adjudication might involve a dispute between a subcontractor and a sub-subcontractor, which could require consent to access from the main contractor in control of a site.

We have touched on the challenge of estimating, at the outset of an adjudication, the time that might be required to prepare and draft the Decision, when the extent of submissions or issues may not be fully known. For this reason, we consider the time that might be required for drafting should be kept under ongoing review throughout the process. By the time submissions have closed, an adjudicator should be in a better position to assess how much time is required and also the state of their diary. If it becomes apparent that the time allowed could be insufficient, our view is that it is better to raise this with the parties sooner rather than later and to seek consent to a revised Decision date. We also think that the adjudicator should briefly explain the reason why the extension is required, e.g. because of an illness, another matter overrunning or simply because the drafting is taking longer than anticipated.

Given that a late Decision will most likely be unenforceable, if the adjudicator considers that there is uncertainty as to whether an extension has been agreed, clarification should be sought from the parties. Otherwise, the adjudicator may not be entitled to payment of their fees, as the following example demonstrates.

RELEVANT CASE LAW

The UK case of *Baldwin & Anor v Pickstock Ltd*[1] concerned a claim by an adjudicator, Mr Baldwin, for payment of his fees in an adjudication in which the defendant was the Referring Party. In the adjudication the adjudicator was obliged to reach his Decision by 20 April 2016. He suggested an extension of time to 20 May 2016 to conclude the adjudication, with a long-stop date of 27 May 2016. The defendant agreed to an extension to 20 May 2016 and made further submissions. The adjudicator then suggested a further extension to 7 June 2016 and, although the defendant did not respond, the other

1 [2017] EWHC 2456 (TCC).

party agreed. On 31 May 2016 the defendant indicated that it had expected a decision by 27 May 2016, and when the defendant refused to agree an extension on 7 June 2016, the adjudicator resigned two days later citing paragraph 9(1) of Part I of the Scheme for Construction Contracts (England & Wales) Regulations 1998, which permits the adjudicator to 'resign at any time on giving notice to the parties'. The adjudicator raised an invoice for his fees of circa £28,000 and directed that they were paid by the defendant in accordance with his terms and conditions. When the defendant did not pay, the adjudicator started proceedings.

The court found that there had been an extension to the date for the adjudicator's Decision to 7 June 2016, but that the Decision date thereafter lapsed, meaning that the adjudicator's resignation on 9 June 2016 had been invalid. As such, the adjudicator's claim for payment of his fees failed.

Another factor to consider when setting the timetable is the number of rounds of submissions. In some cases the applicable adjudication rules may provide for a Response (and may also prescribe a time by which the Response should be served). However, even where no Response is expressly provided, it is fair to say that the expectation is (and the rules of natural justice arguably require) that the Responding Party will have the right to provide a Response. We understand that some practitioners do not routinely provide for a second submission from the Referring Party, which is commonly referred to as a Reply, in their initial directions for timetable. In our experience, it is more likely than not for a Reply to be required. Typically, a Response will include argument or provide evidence that requires comment or rebuttal. For this reason we tend to provide for a Reply in our initial directions.

For submissions beyond the Reply, where we set the timetable in a simple case or where the parties have been unable to agree it in larger and more complex cases, we typically impose a requirement for these further submissions to be the subject of a prior application for permission to serve a further submission. When such an application is received, we tend towards inviting the other side's comment on the request before confirming our decision on it. This is because, while the request may be uncontroversial and agreed to by the other side, this is not always the case, and a decision will then need to be made as to whether to permit further submissions and also to account for any effect on the timetable that has previously been set.

The starting point for permission being granted is whether further comment is necessary from a procedural fairness perspective. An obvious reason to refuse a request is because the adjudicator already knows that the party seeking permission to serve a further submission will be successful in the adjudication, or at least the particular part of the dispute that concerns the further submission. Obviously, to be in a position to know who the successful party will be will require the adjudicator to be on top of the submissions and sufficiently informed of the issues. This will not always be the case, especially in complex cases or where the issues are multifaceted, such that it is not possible to rule out a requirement for further submissions on the basis that the applicant has already 'won'. In such circumstances, it may be appropriate to ask the applicant to identify the specific aspects of the previous submission, or even the particular paragraphs, it wishes to comment on in order to assist the adjudicator in deciding whether to permit a further submission.

Another consideration in deciding whether to permit a further submission is whether it will assist the adjudicator in reaching their Decision. It may be that, after reading the submissions, the adjudicator has unanswered questions, and this might particularly be the case if the parties' cases have developed during the course of the adjudication. If a further submission or submissions are likely to assist the adjudicator in reaching their Decision, then they should be permitted, subject to ensuring that the parties agree to extending the date for the Decision if the adjudicator considers that to be necessary.

In relation to the time required for a further submission, again this is likely to be case specific and dependent on the availability of those required to prepare the submission. However, one also needs to keep an eye on what time period is fair in relation to the time that was available to the other side to prepare and produce its previous submission. For example, a period of time that was longer than the other side had to prepare its previous submission might not appear fair, especially if the scope of the further submission is limited to specific points. It may also be that permission to make a further submission is subject to prior agreement to a period of time for the other side to provide any rebuttal comments in the event that proves necessary.

Although there is no universally accepted convention, the names that we see for submissions in adjudications tend to be as follows.

- Referral: the Referring Party's statement of case and supporting documents/evidence (sometimes referred to as the Referral Notice).
- Response: the Responding Party's responsive submissions and supporting documents/evidence.
- Reply: the Referring Party's responsive submissions to matters arising from the Response.
- Rejoinder: the Responding Party's comments on matters arising from the Reply.
- Surrejoinder: the Referring Party's responsive submissions to matters arising from the Rejoinder.
- Rebutter/Rebuttal: the Responding Party's comments on matters arising from the Surrejoinder.
- Surrebutter/Surrebuttal: the Referring Party's responsive submissions to matters arising from the Rebutter/Rebuttal.

In our experience, submissions up to and including a Rejoinder are common while submissions beyond that are less so. We also increasingly see parties agreeing timetables that provide for a Rejoinder at the outset, perhaps because they realize that a Rejoinder may be inevitable and that it is therefore better to agree a date for one at the outset so that diaries and resources can be planned in advance. Providing for a Rejoinder also means that both parties have an equal number of submissions. In that regard, from time to time we see a Referring Party asserting that it is convention for them to be given 'the last word'. This is presumably on the basis that it reflects the convention in contested litigation or arbitration proceedings, especially in common law/adversarial type proceedings. In our view, there is no such convention in adjudication; the key factor must be whether a further submission is necessary and/or required for the purposes of procedural fairness.

EXAMPLE 3.3: EXAMPLE OF A FAIR AND REASONABLE TIMETABLE ONE OF US HAS PROPOSED IN A LARGE AND COMPLEX ADJUDICATION WHERE THE PARTIES HAVE BEEN UNABLE TO REACH AGREEMENT

Turning to the timetable, I consider a fair and reasonable timetable to be as follows.

- *Response*. Given the size and nature of the disputes, I consider that a period of four weeks for preparation of the Response is reasonable. However, I consider that this period should run from receipt of the Referral supporting documents and, assuming the downloading issues are resolved today, I propose that the period for preparation of the Response commences today, therefore resulting in a submission date of Wednesday 2 March 2022.

- *Reply*. I do not accept the Referring Party's suggestion that it should be provided with the same period for preparation of the Reply that the Responding Party is provided for the Response. However, it will clearly require longer than the one week proposed by the Responding Party. I consider a reasonable submission date for the Reply to be Friday 18 March 2022.

- *Rejoinder*. In my experience of these types of final account dispute, a Rejoinder will inevitably be required, and I consider that it is prudent to make provision for a Rejoinder at this stage of the proceedings. I consider a reasonable submission date to be Friday 25 March 2022.

- *Meeting or site visit*. If I consider a meeting or site visit to be necessary, then I propose to hold it on Friday 2 April 2022. I therefore ask both parties to provisionally set aside this date. Once I have received the Response and read the parties' submissions, I will notify the parties whether I consider a meeting or site visit to be necessary and will provide an agenda if applicable.

- *Decision*. Given the nature and complexity of the dispute I currently anticipate that I am likely to require circa four weeks from

> the close of the submissions to reach my Decision, i.e. until Tuesday 26 April 2022 (accounting for the two Easter bank holidays).
>
> My proposed timetable is dependent on the parties agreeing an extension to the date for my Decision to Tuesday 26 April 2022. I therefore ask the parties to confirm by midday tomorrow whether they agree to extend the date for my Decision to Tuesday 26 April 2022. For the avoidance of doubt, I acknowledge that any such agreement by the Responding Party will be without prejudice to its position as to my jurisdiction.

We have already alluded to the move away from hard copy submissions and supporting documents to electronic soft copies being acceptable. It is therefore worth mentioning that electronic submissions are not free from difficulties. Accordingly, to reiterate what we said in chapter 2, it might be desirable for an adjudicator to include in their directions any restrictions as to the size of attachments sent by email, or to provide for large files to be transmitted via a file transfer portal or to be compressed. Additionally, it might be desirable to limit the file name size as we have sometimes encountered issues with accessing compressed files with large file names. It may also be sensible to direct that documentation is provided in its native form, e.g. spreadsheets or programming files, to assist the adjudicator and the parties when interrogating, using or adapting them (assuming that they have an appropriate license or access to the relevant software). Similarly, we know that some adjudicators may ask for documents to be provided in a machine-readable or searchable format. It may also be sensible to require electronic documents to be indexed and organized within folders, rather than being provided in the electronic equivalent of a paper dump in a 'shopping bag' full of documents. Although this is something that is probably more relevant to the parties (or their representatives), we sometimes find that electronic documents have not been formatted for printing, so if the adjudicator wishes to print documents, it may be helpful to include a direction regarding formatting for printing.

One final point to make regarding the provision of electronic documents relates to cyber security and data protection issues. Although we are not experts in the area, we are conscious that some of the data we receive might be of a personal nature and/or commercially sensitive, or even subject to privacy regulations. It is therefore important to ensure that any documentation provided is sufficiently protected from being accessed or used by unauthorized persons. On a related point, measures or systems for destroying documents after the adjudication has concluded might need to be put in place.

EXTENSION OF TIME REQUESTS

Having set the initial directions for the timetable, an adjudicator may be faced with requests for more time to provide a submission. This can sometimes be immediately after initial directions have been set or after a timetable has been agreed by the parties. Again, the principles of procedural fairness fall to be considered.

When receiving an application for an extension of time for submissions, in most instances we will invite comment from the other party. Circumstances where it might not be necessary to invite comment include where the time required is short and can be accommodated within the existing timetable without affecting the cut-off date for submissions or the Decision date, or where it is possible to afford the other party a commensurate or corresponding period of additional time for a subsequent submission. For example, the request might be to extend the time for submission from, say 5 p.m. to midnight as a result of difficulties in collating or finalizing a submission or supporting documents.

Assuming comment is invited, as for the situation when addressing a request to serve a further submission, the request may be uncontroversial or uncontested. In the event it is contested, though, a decision will need to be made as to whether to extend the deadline for the relevant submission, taking into account the specific circumstances (and the reason for the request) and the extent to which it is possible to accommodate it within the existing timetable. If it is not possible to accommodate the request within the existing timetable, an adjudicator will need to obtain consent to extend the date for the Decision in order to facilitate it. Here, the adjudicator's view on what constitutes a reasonable and fair extension may assist the opposing party's decision to agree to a revised Decision date. Ultimately, if consent to a revised Decision date is not forthcoming, it may be appropriate to limit the extension of time to a date that still enables the adjudicator to reach their Decision within the existing timetable, especially if there is sufficient latitude within the time the adjudicator has and they are comfortable with allowing themselves a shorter period to reach and draft their Decision after the final submission.

CONCURRENT/SERIAL ADJUDICATIONS

Concurrent and serial adjudications between the parties are not unheard of. The extent to which it is permissible to refer different disputes arising under one contract to a single adjudicator at the same time may depend on the legislation and the applicable adjudication rules. For example, in the United Kingdom, where the adjudication provisions of the Scheme for Construction Contracts (England and Wales) Regulations 1998 ('the Scheme')[2] apply, the parties' consent may be required for a single adjudicator to act in concurrent adjudications. Absent such consent, it might be that there are a number of concurrent adjudications involving different adjudicators.

Where it is permissible for a single adjudicator to act on concurrent adjudications between the same parties, the question is then whether that is desirable. On the one hand, it might ensure consistency. On the other, it might lengthen the overall timetable on account of the burden on the adjudicator. However, it is not only the burden on the adjudicator that should be considered, but also the burden on the parties, and particularly that on the Responding Party. It should be remembered that the Referring Party typically elects what dispute it will refer to adjudication and when the referral will be made. The Referring Party may have been preparing its case and marshalling its evidence for some time and – irrespective of whether a single adjudicator is appointed or different adjudicators are appointed – the Responding Party may be placed in an onerous position. In our view, an adjudicator should factor such difficulties into their timetable. In some circumstances it may be that the appropriate course of action is to resign or elect not to proceed at all if a Referring Party is not prepared to agree to an extended timetable that the adjudicator considers fair. Again, our view is that the timetable prescribed by statute or by the contract is subordinate to a requirement to comply with the rules of natural justice.

2 Separate 'Schemes' exist for Scotland and Northern Ireland.

Although rare, we also have experience of concurrent adjudications between different parties arising in connection with a single project. For example, a dispute between an employer and a main contractor might concern alleged defects in relation to specialist works undertaken by a number of different subcontractors who are all employed under separate subcontracts. Sometimes those subcontracts may provide for a type of 'joinder' or 'consolidation', but even without such provisions a main contractor might seek to have the same adjudicator acting to ensure consistency. In such circumstances care needs to be taken to ensure procedural fairness, and this might require the parties' agreement for documents in their adjudication to be shared with non-parties in the related adjudications. This is to avoid any suggestion that the adjudicator could have been influenced by submissions or documents provided in a separate adjudication that a party did not have the opportunity to comment on.

Serial adjudications, i.e. adjudications arising under the same contract between the same parties but following a previous Decision or Decisions, throw up other challenges. This is true even when the same adjudicator has acted previously but is more so where different adjudicators have acted before. A key characteristic of adjudication is that Decisions are temporarily binding on the parties (and therefore in subsequent adjudications) until either otherwise agreed by the parties or reversed or 'trumped' by a tribunal with higher authority, such as a court or arbitrator.

Parties will sometimes disagree about the extent to which a previous Decision (or part of a Decision) is binding. For example, does an adjudicator's reasoning or findings in relation to certain issues form part of the binding part of the Decision, or is it just the dispositive or final section of the Decision (i.e. where the orders and declarations are set out) that is binding? Parties might also argue that a dispute that has been referred to an adjudicator has already been decided either in whole or in part previously, and that the subsequent adjudicator is therefore either prevented or constrained as to what they are able to decide in a subsequent adjudication. In order to form a conclusion and avoid trespassing on a previous Decision, the adjudicator might have to review and consider the submissions and arguments that were advanced in the previous adjudication, as the most important factor will invariably be to determine what was decided in the previous Decision.

RELEVANT CASE LAW

A summary of the general principles applicable under UK law in circumstances where there are arguments of overlap in serial adjudications can be found in the case of *Sudlows Ltd v Global Switch Estates 1 Ltd*,[3] in which Lord Justice Coulson, who gave the leading judgment in the Court of Appeal, stated:

> '55. … I consider that there are three over-arching principles to be applied by an adjudicator, or an enforcing court, when considering arguments of overlap.
>
> 56. The first is that the purpose of construction adjudication is not easy always to reconcile with serial adjudication (…). If the parties to a construction contract do engage in serial adjudication, and then inevitably get drawn into debates about whether a particular dispute has already been decided, the need for speed and the importance of at least temporary finality mean that the adjudicator (and, if necessary, the court on enforcement) should be encouraged to give a robust and common sense answer to the issue. It should not be a complex question of interpretation of documents and citation of authority.
>
> 57. The second is the need to look at what the first adjudicator actually decided to see if the second adjudicator has impinged on the earlier decision (*Quietfield, Harding v Paice, Hitachi*). Of course it can be relevant to consider the adjudication notice, the referral notice and so on, but what matters for the purposes of s. 108 and the paragraphs of the Scheme noted above, is what it was, in reality, that the adjudicator decided. It is that which cannot be re-adjudicated. The form and content of the documentation with which he was provided is of lesser relevance and, as was pointed out in *Harding v Paice* and *Hitachi*, can be misleading.
>
> 58. The third critical principle is the need for flexibility. That is the purpose of a test of fact and degree. It is to prevent a party from re-adjudicating a claim (or a defence) on which they

---

3 [2023] EWCA Civ 813.

> have unequivocally lost (*HG Construction, Benfield*), but to ensure that what is essentially a new claim or a new defence is not shut out. …
>
> 59. Whilst I accept that it is not an invariable guide, one way of at least testing whether the correct approach has been adopted is to consider whether, if the second adjudication is allowed to continue, it would or might lead to a result which is fundamentally incompatible with the result in the first adjudication. If in that second adjudication, one or other of the parties is asking the adjudicator to do something that is diametrically opposed to that which the first adjudicator decided, then that may be an indication that what they are seeking to do is impermissible.'

INSOLVENT PARTIES

Adjudications sometimes involve a party who is insolvent. The extent to which it is permissible for an insolvent party to refer a dispute to adjudication, or for a solvent party to refer a dispute to adjudication against an insolvent party, will depend on the particular legislation and jurisdiction. Specifically, permission may be required from the insolvency practitioner (or the supervising court) to enable a matter to proceed. In the event of permission being given, the question of whether the insolvent party wishes to take part arises. We address the issues that may arise when one party does not take part in an adjudication in chapter 7, so we do not cover that situation here, but if the insolvent party does wish to take part, an undertaking may be required from the insolvency practitioner that they have sufficient means to pay the adjudicator's fees. If they do not have sufficient means, the question arises of whether it would be procedurally fair to proceed. In such circumstances, and assuming the insolvent party was the Responding Party, it may be appropriate to ask the Referring Party whether they still wish to proceed. Although this might seem odd, we are aware that there might still be a benefit to having an adjudicator's Decision against an insolvent party, e.g. there might be a guarantee or bond in place that responds to an adjudicator's Decision. A Referring Party may therefore be prepared to incur costs and undertake to pay the adjudicator's fees in order to obtain such a benefit.

A situation in which the insolvent party is referring the dispute to adjudication is slightly different, in that, unless the insolvent party (or the insolvency practitioner) has provided an undertaking that it has the means to pay the adjudicator's fees, there is greater potential for procedural unfairness because the Responding Party may be obliged to pay the adjudicator's fees irrespective of whether it is successful. Where no undertaking is provided from the insolvency practitioner, we do not consider it appropriate for an adjudicator to proceed. That said, our experience of insolvency practitioners is that, where undertakings have been provided and a referral to adjudication has been unsuccessful, our fees have always been paid promptly.

CHAPTER 4

Jurisdictional challenges

In a process that affords one party to a contract the unilateral right to refer a dispute to adjudication, it is perhaps inevitable that the party on the receiving end of a reference may seek to avoid the proceedings or an unfavourable outcome. Consequently, a practice has developed whereby a party will seek to contest the adjudicator's right to act or to challenge the extent of their role. This has resulted in what is commonly termed jurisdictional challenges, and they are the subject of this chapter.

As jurisdictional challenges can be commonplace, it is important that an adjudicator is well versed in the applicable law surrounding such challenges. As this book is not jurisdiction specific (in terms of a particular country or state), we do not cover the applicable law here. What we do cover is the types of challenge that may arise and how to deal with them. In our view, dealing with challenges is an integral part of the role of an adjudicator, as well as being one of the most challenging.

TYPES OF JURISDICTIONAL CHALLENGE

Although challenges to jurisdiction will be fact specific, in broad terms challenges fall into two categories: threshold and internal. A threshold jurisdictional challenge is one which goes to the underlying right for the adjudication to proceed and for the right of the adjudicator to act. To use a sporting analogy, is it right for the 'referee' to be on the pitch at all. An internal jurisdictional challenge is one that does not go to the underlying right for the adjudication to take place or for the adjudicator to act, but instead concerns the ambit of the adjudication or the extent of the adjudicator's role. Returning to our sporting analogy, it is the limit of the referee's powers, e.g. the ability to discipline players or team members during the contest. We address each type of challenge in turn.

When we think of threshold challenges, it is useful to consider the criteria that need to be satisfied in order for an adjudication to take place and for an adjudicator to act. Some of the criteria will be substantive, e.g. there must be a dispute arising under (or, if applicable, in connection with) a qualifying contract, and others will be administrative, e.g. relating to the correct sequence and steps that need to be followed in order for an appointment to be effective. If the criteria have not been satisfied, it can be said that there is no right for a particular adjudication to proceed. The types of threshold jurisdictional challenges we have seen are listed below.

Substantive

(i) No qualifying construction contract.

(ii) No contract (at all).

(iii) Incorrect party names, e.g. one or more parties to the adjudication are not the party or parties to the contract.

(iv) No dispute.

(v) More than one dispute.

(vi) The dispute that has been referred is different to the one that was notified.

(vii) The dispute referred relates to a claim that is time-barred.

(viii) The dispute has already been decided by a previous adjudicator.

(ix) The legislation prevents the type of dispute from being referred before a precondition has been satisfied, e.g. in the United Kingdom, the courts have held that a party cannot refer a dispute on the 'true value' of the works in respect of a particular payment cycle unless it has satisfied any payment obligations that may have arisen as a consequence of the payment notification regime.

Administrative

(i) An incorrect procedure regarding sequence and/or timing for appointment has been followed.

(ii) The nominating body or authority was incorrect.

(iii) The adjudicator does not possess the prescribed qualifications.

(iv) The adjudicator has a conflict of interest.

Internal jurisdictional challenges typically concern the extent of the matter that has been referred or the decisions or declarations that the adjudicator has been asked to make. In contrast to threshold jurisdictional challenges, these types of challenge may be raised by either party. Threshold challenges are generally advanced by the Responding Party, who is often seeking to avoid the adjudication process altogether or, at the very least, to delay it. Conversely, internal challenges are not necessarily intended to stop the process altogether but to limit the scope of the adjudication or the adjudicator's remit in some way. For example, a Responding Party may seek to advance a counterclaim and/or seek certain redress in its Response, and a Referring Party may then object to the counterclaim being considered or to the adjudicator's power to grant the redress sought. Further, a Responding Party may accept that a Referring Party has the right to refer part of the subject matter to adjudication, but not all of it, and they might consequently seek to advance a challenge to limit the scope of what the adjudicator can address. For example, a Responding Party could argue that part of the matter referred had already been decided by a previous adjudicator.

The types of internal jurisdictional challenges we have seen include where

- the matter does not fall within the scope of the dispute that has been referred to adjudication;

- the adjudicator does not have the power to grant the redress sought;
- there is no dispute concerning part of the claim; or
- part of the dispute has already been decided by a previous adjudicator.

AN ADJUDICATOR'S POWER TO ADDRESS JURISDICTIONAL CHALLENGES

Before addressing how an adjudicator deals with a jurisdictional challenge, we address the question of where an adjudicator gets the power to address jurisdictional challenges from, and also the effect of an adjudicator's conclusion on their jurisdiction. Unlike in arbitration, which has the concept of ***kompetenz-kompetenz***,[1] most legislation does not provide that an adjudicator has the power to rule on their jurisdiction. Thus, unless there is an express power included in the applicable adjudication rules, an adjudicator does not have the power to rule on the extent of their jurisdiction, whether in a final sense or a temporarily binding one. Such power would typically be vested in the supervising court (or potentially the arbitration tribunal). We are aware that some adjudication rules do seek to confer such a power, e.g. those published by the Technology and Construction Solicitors Association (TECSA) in England and Wales, albeit even then it is still arguably possible for a court to review the adjudicator's findings on jurisdiction. More typically though, the rules are silent as to the powers that an adjudicator has to rule on their own jurisdiction.

Although it is unusual, on some occasions we have experienced the parties agreeing that the adjudicator should reach a decision on a jurisdictional challenge and that they are happy to be bound by it in the same way that they may be bound by a Decision in relation to a substantive dispute. The parties can therefore be taken to have expressly agreed that the adjudicator has the power to consider the challenge and reach a decision.

Where the legislation or adjudication rules are silent on the adjudicator's powers or where the parties have not expressly agreed that the adjudicator has the power, then the next thing to consider is whether

1 The power of the arbitrator to determine their own jurisdiction.

there is any guidance from the supervising court in the relevant legal jurisdiction as to what an adjudicator should do when faced with a jurisdictional challenge. In the United Kingdom, it is clear that the courts consider that the adjudicator is under an obligation to satisfy themselves that they have jurisdiction, either as a result of a challenge or of their own volition. Thus, it can be said that, in the United Kingdom, the adjudicator has the power to reach a non-binding conclusion on their jurisdiction as a matter of 'common law' (i.e. judge-made law).

In practical terms, absent an express provision or the parties' express agreement, it can be seen that the source of a power to address a jurisdictional challenge could stem from the obligation of an adjudicator to conduct the adjudication in a procedurally fair manner. However, this assumes that there is a right to adjudicate in the first place. The situation may differ in circumstances where there is no right to adjudicate. In such a situation, it may arguably be the case that there is some kind of contractual relationship between the party who applied for the adjudicator's appointment and the 'adjudicator' who was appointed, but the relationship between the person appointed as the 'adjudicator' and the party making a jurisdictional challenge may differ, especially if the challenging party has not accepted the validity of the appointment. In such circumstances, there may nevertheless be an obligation to address the challenge and to reach a conclusion, although whether or not that arises from a contractual relationship is perhaps a moot point.

Unless there are express provisions that provide for an adjudicator's conclusion or decision on jurisdiction to be binding on the parties, then the extent to which such a decision is binding may depend on whether or not the parties have expressly reserved their position either before or after the adjudicator has been asked to consider the challenge. For example, where the party making the challenge makes it clear that they do not confer upon the adjudicator the power to determine their own jurisdiction, then the adjudicator's conclusion is unlikely to be binding. This is also likely to be the case where, after an adjudicator has investigated their jurisdiction and concluded they do have jurisdiction, the party who made the challenge continues to reserve their position when taking further steps or continuing to participate in the adjudication.

To a certain extent, the question of whether an adjudicator's conclusion or decision on jurisdiction is binding as a result of the parties' conduct is not something that needs to concern the adjudicator. However, there is a school of thought that suggests that, if a ruling on jurisdiction is a procedural issue and not a substantive one, the rules of natural justice do not apply. If that is correct, then, conceptually, there may be a distinction between the approach to be adopted depending on whether or not the decision on jurisdiction is binding. In practice, however, the approach adopted by an adjudicator when addressing a jurisdictional challenge is unlikely to differ.

HOW TO DEAL WITH JURISDICTIONAL CHALLENGES

How adjudicators deal with jurisdictional challenges will depend both on whether the challenge is threshold or internal and on the timing of the challenge. Key considerations will be the effect of an unsuccessful challenge on the timetable and also the effect on costs (i.e. the adjudicator's fees and also the parties' own costs) of a challenge being successful.

Although it is less common, some challenges occur prior to the date the Referral is served. Even less common are challenges prior to the nomination or appointment of the adjudicator. Clearly, if the challenge is prior to the nomination or appointment, there is arguably nothing for the adjudicator to do. For example, it may be that the challenge is made to the ANA/ANB. In such circumstances, the ANA/ANB may seek your views. Our thoughts are that if such a challenge appears valid and/or could be easily rectified, it may save time and unnecessary effort if the ANA/ANB liaises with the applicant in order to resolve any issue.

If a challenge is made following an appointment or nomination but before a Referral is served, the question of whether to address the challenge before or after the Referral is filed then arises. There is a school of thought that holds that the adjudicator's appointment is not complete until the Referral is served, but we do not agree. Although the Referral may trigger the obligation to reach a Decision, the adjudicator's function is not restricted to the production of the Decision. Indeed, some consider that the case management function can be more challenging than reaching and drafting the Decision. However, irrespective of whether the appointment of the adjudicator is effected before or after the Referral is served, we consider that, save for one exception, it is better to address any jurisdictional challenge that has been lodged after the Referral is served. This is because the Referring Party may elect not to serve at all, meaning any time spent by the adjudicator will have been wasted and/

or result in unnecessary costs being incurred. The one exception is when there is a challenge based on a conflict of interest that an adjudicator considers to be valid. In such circumstances, our view is that the correct course of action is to stand down so that an alternative appointment can be made. Ordinarily, however, we would acknowledge the challenge and invite the Referring Party to provide any comments it wishes to make on the challenge at the same time as it serves the Referral.

If the challenge is made after the Referral is served, then, as for pre-Referral challenges, we would invite the Referring Party's comment. Depending on the extent or complexity of the challenge, we might set a deadline for response (typically a day) or, alternatively, we might ask the Referring Party to confirm when it will be in a position to provide its comments. This is so time can be set aside in order to address both the challenge and the responsive comments. Once the responsive comments have been received it may be that further comments are invited or received (we find that the party making the challenge will typically make further submissions).

If the challenge is a threshold one, then it will need to be addressed quickly. This is because, if it is deemed to be valid, it could bring the adjudication to an end and avoid the Responding Party (and arguably both parties) incurring unnecessary costs. Conversely, if not considered valid, addressing the challenge quickly could avoid unnecessary delay. In that regard, although a timetable may have already been set, it may be that the question of timetable is deferred pending the adjudicator's conclusion on jurisdiction. In any event, there is a need for a decision on jurisdiction to be made and then communicated to the parties.

In order to investigate the challenge, the adjudicator may have to consider case law or authorities, facts, documentary evidence and the parties' competing submissions. There are arguably no prescribed rules as to who has the burden of making out its case in respect of a jurisdictional challenge. However, the key question for the adjudicator is whether they are satisfied that they have jurisdiction. If they conclude that they do, then the answer should be communicated promptly. If time permits, our view is that reasons for the conclusion should be given, even if they are brief. However, if there is not enough time, it may be preferrable for the adjudicator to advise of their conclusion with a note that reasons will follow. In such circumstances we consider it best to provide reasons before the Decision, but if doing so is not practicable, we would suggest that the Decision provides the reasons for the conclusion.

EXAMPLE 4.1: EXAMPLE OF AN EMAIL COMMUNICATING A NON-BINDING CONCLUSION ON JURISDICTION

Dear all,
I have now had an opportunity to consider the parties' submissions on my jurisdiction and I set out my non-binding conclusion below.

Parties' submissions

The Responding Party contends that the dispute that the Referring Party seeks to have decided in this adjudication is not as stated in the Notice of Adjudication ('the Notice'), namely, the dispute concerning the true value of the Referring Party's Application for Payment 22 dated 18 July 2023 (AFP22), but rather a purported dispute concerning the claim set out under cover of a letter from Westminster QS Limited ('Westminster') dated 3 August 2023, received by the Responding Party on 4 August 2023. The Responding Party notes that this comprises a 93-page report and 18 lever arch files of supporting documents, and that it has not had sufficient time to consider it such that no dispute has arisen regarding this claim. The Responding Party also contends that, given the date this claim was submitted, it does not fall for consideration until the August application: that is, AFP23. The Responding Party therefore submits that 'what has been referred to you is not capable of being referred to adjudication at this time', and it has therefore invited me to resign.

The Referring Party submits that the dispute referred in this adjudication concerns the true value of AFP22, and that Westminster's submission of 3 August 2023 comprises further evidence in support of its claim for an extension of time and additional costs, which was initially submitted in early March 2023 and which has been the subject of a number of meetings and letter/email exchanges between the parties. The Referring Party refers me to *Cantillon Ltd v Urvasco Ltd* ([2008] EWHC 282 (TCC)) in support of its case. The Referring Party therefore maintains that I have jurisdiction to proceed with this adjudication.

My non-binding conclusion

I acknowledge that much of the Notice and the Referral make reference to Westminster's submission of 3 August 2023, but I do not accept that the adjudication concerns this submission, rather than AFP22, as contended by the Responding Party. Rather, I agree with the Referring Party that it is clear from the Notice and the Referral that the dispute referred concerns the true value of AFP22, and that Westminster's 3 August 2023 submission comprises further arguments and evidence in support of the Referring Party's true value claim, and in particular the disputed additional costs. I note in this regard that the Responding Party has not referred me to any heads of claim in Westminster's 3 August 2023 submission that have not been claimed in AFP22.

The dispute regarding the true value of AFP22 evidently arose no later than 13 August 2023, when the Responding Party issued its Pay Less Notice, and therefore the further arguments and evidence were submitted nine days prior to the crystallization of the dispute. In any event, as noted by the Referring Party, it is well established law that a 'claiming party is not limited to the arguments, contentions and evidence put forward by it before the dispute crystallised' (per Akenhead J at paragraph 55 of his judgment in *Cantillon Ltd v Urvasco*), and therefore the Referring Party could have relied on Westminster's 3 August 2023 submission even if it had been submitted after 13 August 2023.

Even if I am wrong and the dispute referred concerns Westminster's 3 August 2023 submission, rather than AFP22, in the circumstances I consider that a dispute has crystallized regarding that submission. The Referring Party's claim has evidently been in existence since early March 2023 and has been the subject of a number of meetings and letter/email exchanges between the parties; the gist of the claim is therefore clearly well known to the Responding Party, and Westminster's 3 August 2023 submission was in direct response to questions raised by the Responding Party. I therefore consider that the Responding Party's silence for the two weeks following submission of the claim on 4 August 2023 was sufficient to give rise to a dispute by the time the Notice was issued on 18 August 2023.

It therefore follows that my non-binding conclusion is that I have jurisdiction in this adjudication, and I therefore decline the Responding Party's request for me to resign.

However, I ask the Referring Party to note that, although I accept that it is entitled to rely on Westminster's 3 August 2023 submission as evidence to support its claim concerning the true value of AFP22 and that, even if it constitutes a new claim, sufficient time passed before the issue of the Notice for a dispute to crystallise, given the volume of information submitted, the Responding Party must be provided with adequate time to prepare the Response in this adjudication, in order to ensure the process is fair.

We are aware that some adjudicators may communicate their conclusion on jurisdiction in a separate document, almost akin to a 'decision' on jurisdiction. Although this may be appropriate where the adjudicator has the power to rule on their jurisdiction and/or where the time and cost of doing so is not excessive, the approach we tend to adopt is to set out our conclusion and reasons in either an email or a letter including numbered paragraphs. If we conclude that we have jurisdiction, we would then incorporate the content of the email or letter into the body of our Decision within a section entitled 'Jurisdiction'.

If the adjudicator concludes that they do not have jurisdiction, the answer, again, needs to be communicated promptly. However, as it is now unlikely that there will be a Decision, reasons should be given so that the Referring Party understands why the adjudicator has reached that conclusion. When communicating the conclusion, we would ask the Responding Party to confirm whether it still wishes for us to resign. This is because it may be that the Responding Party is prepared to waive its challenge, e.g. if the jurisdictional issue can be easily resolved and it is inevitable that a new adjudication will follow, if the real motivation for the challenge was to secure a longer period to prepare the Response, or if the Responding Party is seeking to expand the scope of the adjudication to encompass a counterclaim. However, if the Responding Party confirms that it still maintains its challenge and seeks the adjudicator's resignation, then the adjudicator should stand down at that point. We would then raise an invoice for the time spent investigating the challenge. Although we would ask the Referring Party to make payment, we would nevertheless still confirm that, in line with our terms, the parties are joint and severally liable. Although the obligation to pay may differ between jurisdictions, in the United Kingdom the courts have made it clear that a party making a successful challenge is still nevertheless liable to pay an adjudicator for their time investigating the challenge.

Challenges may sometimes be included in the Response itself. In such circumstances, the requirement for a speedy investigation may be less acute than if the challenge had been made earlier. This is on the basis that, at this stage, the Responding Party has already incurred the expense of preparing and serving a Response. Nevertheless, if the challenge is a threshold one, it may be prudent to address it as a discrete point and in advance of any substantive Reply being served in order to avoid unnecessary costs. However, if the Referring Party is content to address the challenge at the same time it serves a Reply, then we would not object. Once the comments have been received, we would address the challenge in the same way as outlined above, communicating our decision promptly, with reasons if it is practicable to do so.

The question of whether an adjudicator should raise jurisdictional issues of their own volition sometimes arises. In our view, the right answer to this question differs depending on the experience or status of the parties and/or their representatives. For example, an unrepresented consumer who is a residential owner-occupier may not be aware that their contract may not qualify for adjudication. In such circumstances, if the adjudicator is concerned about whether there is a right to adjudicate (and about whether the adjudicator will be entitled to a fee), our view is that it would be appropriate to ask the parties to confirm why and/or whether they are content for the adjudication to proceed. Conversely, if both parties are large commercial entities and are represented by experienced lawyers well versed in construction law and adjudication practice, it may be acceptable to leave the parties to raise any challenges as they see fit. That said, if we did have a genuine concern about the validity of our appointment such that we did not feel we could proceed with a clear conscience, we would invite comment to avoid any criticism at a later date.

If the challenge is an internal one, the key consideration will be whether addressing the challenge early could avoid unnecessary cost. For example, if an adjudicator agreed that certain matters included in the Referral (or Response) did not fall within the scope of their jurisdiction, then communicating that view early would avoid a party having to address those matters in their subsequent submissions. However, if the time and effort required to address the matter in issue is likely to be minimal in the context of the wider dispute, it may be best to allow the other party to address the challenge within their substantive submissions.

Ideally, the conclusion on an internal jurisdictional challenge (and the reasons for that conclusion) will have been communicated in advance of the Decision itself. This is so that the parties are made aware of the conclusion in advance, which may be essential so that the parties can tailor their submissions to suit, and also to avoid potential breaches of natural justice, as the following case example demonstrates.

RELEVANT CASE LAW

The UK case of *PC Harrington Contractors Ltd v Systech International Ltd*[2] arose from three adjudications between PC Harrington and one of its subcontractors, Tyroddy Construction Limited, concerning three different subcontracts. Tyroddy sought payment of outstanding retention, and one of PC Harrington's defences was that Tyroddy's works should be revalued, and that such revaluation meant that no retention was payable. The adjudicator concluded that he did not have jurisdiction to consider this defence, but he did not give the parties the opportunity to comment on this conclusion, which was not communicated until he issued his Decision. PC Harrington therefore obtained declarations from the Technology and Construction Court (TCC) that the three Decisions were unenforceable due to breaches of natural justice.

The adjudicator's firm, Systech, commenced proceedings to recover the adjudicator's outstanding fees. Systech was awarded the fees in the TCC but that was overturned by the Court of Appeal, who held that the adjudicator's entitlement to be paid accrues upon the giving of an enforceable Decision. Importantly, though, the Court of Appeal drew a distinction with the situation where an adjudicator has made their non-binding conclusion during the course of the adjudication and has advised the parties of that conclusion. In particular, at paragraph 44 of the judgment Lord Justice Davis stated:

> 'As to the special situation arising in an adjudication where one of the parties raises a challenge on jurisdiction before a decision is reached and then, having received the adjudicator's ruling on jurisdiction, elects that the adjudicator should proceed to a decision, that situation is in my view correctly addressed by Ramsey J at paragraphs 76 to 79 of his judgment in *Linnett v Halliwells*

---

2 [2012] EWCA Civ 1371.

LLP [2009] EWHC 319 (TCC), [2009] BLR 312. The adjudicator's fees are then – subject of course to any express terms agreed – payable even if the Court subsequently were to declare the initial challenge to the jurisdiction to have been well-founded.'

However, it may not always be possible to communicate a conclusion on jurisdiction prior to issuing the Decision. For example, perhaps the timing of the challenge is such that there is no time to address it in advance, or it could be that the determination of the challenge is inextricably linked to the determination of the substantive issues. In such circumstances, it might be the case that the determination and conclusion on the internal challenge could be communicated within the Decision itself.

One situation that we sometimes come across is where a threshold jurisdictional challenge also represents a substantive issue or defence. An example of this may be where a party argues that no contract was formed and/or that the contract that was formed is not the one advocated by the Referring Party such that a claim should be dismissed. When faced with this type of challenge it may be that the appropriate means of dealing with it is to allow the parties to make their submissions in the conventional manner and for the adjudicator to address it in their Decision.

CHAPTER 5

Submissions and evidence

Irrespective of whether an adjudication takes place in an adversarial or inquisitorial context, the adjudicator will be required to receive, assimilate and assess submissions and evidence provided by the parties. In this chapter we discuss the types of submission and evidence that can be encountered, as well as addressing how to deal with requests for further submissions and/or for evidence to be produced. We also address how to deal with 'without prejudice' or 'privileged' material.

TYPES OF SUBMISSION

Submissions can be characterized as the arguments advanced by the parties in support of their case. In broad terms, there are two forms of submission: written and oral. Generally, the most common form of submissions received in adjudication is written. However, if an adjudicator elects to convene a meeting or 'hearing', it is possible that there may also be oral submissions.

Written submissions will generally be presented as part of the formal documentation submitted in accordance with the adjudicator's procedural directions and timetable. Although simultaneous submissions are not unheard of, in our experience they are not common in construction adjudication. What is more typical is sequential submissions, starting with the Referral document and followed by responsive submissions set out in a Response, a Reply, etc.

There is no prescribed form of written submissions, and the quality of the submissions an adjudicator may receive can therefore vary. Good submissions should set out an explanation of the dispute in a clear and logical manner. They should include the relevant background and identification of the issues between the parties, and they should explain why that party's position is considered to be correct and should be followed. Such submissions should refer to the relevant provisions of the contract between the parties, they should set out and explain the relevant law, they should refer to the evidence relied upon and then say how the relevant facts and relevant law lead to the conclusion that supports the relief sought. Finally, they should set out the relief or redress that is being sought.

As well as setting out any positive position, responsive submissions will need to comment on the opposing preceding submissions. As submissions progress, good submissions will be restricted to new matters or issues that have not already been addressed in prior submissions. Unfortunately, we sometimes find that subsequent submissions become repetitive and, rather than being narrow and focused, they can end up as composite submissions that can unnecessarily add to the adjudicator's workload. For this reason, it might be sensible for an adjudicator to make it clear in their initial directions that submissions beyond the Response should be restricted to matters not already addressed previously.

In our view, it is important for the adjudicator to plan and to make time available to undertake an initial review of the submissions at the times they are due to be submitted. This will enable the adjudicator to gain an understanding of the dispute and the issues between the parties in a timely manner, and it should help the adjudicator in a number of ways. First, it should enable the adjudicator to identify any points that may require immediate clarification or action (including any difficulties with accessing electronic documents). Second, it should better equip the adjudicator to address any requests for further submissions or requests for documents (as they will have a better understanding of what may be relevant). Third, it should assist the adjudicator in formulating the issues at an early stage. Finally, it should enable the adjudicator to assess how much time is likely to be needed to reach and prepare their Decision, and therefore to decide whether the time already allowed is likely to be sufficient.

Ideally, there will be adequate time to read the written submissions and supporting information in full shortly after the submissions are served, but sometimes the extent of the submissions and/or the adjudicator's other commitments are such that this is not possible, or it may not be a good use of time. For example, spending hours reading complex expert reports and the like when they are served may not be worthwhile if an extended timetable has been agreed. This is because it is usually necessary, in our experience, to read them again when we come to refer to them some weeks later. In such circumstances, we still think that the 'head' submission documents need to be read and that any supporting documents should be reviewed, even if just to get a feel for the nature, content and volume of the documentation that might need to be reviewed and considered in more detail as part of the process of preparing the Decision.

As the adjudicator works through the written submissions it is useful to make a note (mental or otherwise) of what is common ground or agreed and what is not. It is also useful to make a note of what the adjudicator considers the issues to be and what questions will need to be determined. As the adjudication progresses, the adjudicator will, if time permits, be able to consider the supporting documents in more detail, and this might identify whether any further clarification or additional information is required.

As we already said, oral submissions are less common in our experience, but they may nevertheless be helpful in certain circumstances. For example, if the written submissions are unclear, it may be helpful to have them explained orally. Further, if the parties are legally represented and there are complex legal issues, it may assist the adjudicator's understanding to have the legal representatives talk them through the relevant law and legal principles. In the event the adjudicator elects to receive oral submissions, it is important for the adjudicator to keep in mind the principles of natural justice and, in particular, the need for each party to have a reasonable opportunity to respond to the other party's case. This may be easier to monitor with written submissions than with oral submissions on account of the fact that the oral submissions or argument may be presented for the first time in a meeting or hearing. This could lead to a situation where the opposing party may not be in a position to respond immediately. In such circumstances, it may be appropriate to either adjourn for a short period or to allow the opposing party to provide any responsive comments in writing at a later date.

The other important point in respect of oral submissions is that, unlike written submissions, the adjudicator may not be provided with a written note of those submissions. The adjudicator will therefore need to plan how to record the oral submissions they receive. We address how that could be done in chapter 6, which deals with how meetings and hearings may be conducted.

TYPES OF EVIDENCE: FACTUAL EVIDENCE

In broad terms, the type of evidence provided to an adjudicator will be either fact based or opinion based. Factual evidence typically comprises contemporaneous documents or the recollection of witnesses with knowledge of the subject matter.

The most obvious form of documentary evidence that may be required is that which evidences the underlying contract. Where a contract is evidenced or recorded in writing, the contract documentation is typically provided (or at least those parts that are considered to be relevant are). Where the contract relates to a large, complex or major project, the volume of contract documentation can be significant. Other documentary evidence that may be provided includes that produced contemporaneously. In the modern era of electronic communications, as well as the relevant attachments and correspondence, this may include emails and other electronic communications, such as copies of text messages. Attachments may take the form of letters, applications for payments, spreadsheets, reports, records of progress, minutes of meetings, programmes, drawings, timesheets, invoices, payslips, accounting records, bank statements, etc.

Other contemporaneous evidence that may be provided can be in the form of photographs, videos and audio files. If produced in digital form, the size of the files can be significant. Audio files are sometimes accompanied by transcripts, and we have also encountered timelapse videos, which are sometimes used to demonstrate the state of progress at a particular date or the sequence of work.

In our experience, it has sometimes been necessary to interrogate the documentary evidence provided in order to identify whether it is authentic and/or whether it has been altered. This is not always a straightforward exercise, and it may require some explanation or involve expert evidence in order to explain apparent anomalies or confirm whether or not an electronic communication was sent or received, either at all or at a particular time. This may also involve an inspection of a computer or device in situ. The necessity to inspect documentary evidence may not in fact be restricted to digitally produced files: documents produced in handwritten form, e.g. a note taken at a meeting or the original copy of a timesheet or daywork sheet or invoice, or those that have been signed sometimes need to be assessed to establish their veracity.

Other instances in which it might be necessary to inspect evidence on a computer or other device in situ is where that evidence is confidential or is on a database that cannot easily be condensed into a manageable document to be attached to an adjudication submission. For example, main contractors often use databases to record costs, for accounting purposes, etc., and where the contents of the database are used to support a claim we are sometimes invited to undertake an inspection of the database at the main contractor's office, together with the other party.

As well as documents that have been produced during the currency of a project, the parties may produce evidence prepared after the event. To a certain extent, this type of evidence may be 'contemporaneous', in the sense it was produced prior to the adjudication, but it is helpful for an adjudicator to keep in mind that, perhaps in contrast to truly contemporaneous evidence, the purpose of documents that were prepared after a dispute has arisen will differ, i.e. they may have been prepared specifically for the adjudication and may therefore have been influenced by the desire to succeed in the proceedings. In our experience, truly contemporaneous evidence often carries the most weight.

It has increasingly become the norm in the United Kingdom and Ireland for parties to provide witness statements in support of their cases. Unlike court proceedings, there are no prescribed rules for the form and content of witness statements. Although we know of one UK adjudicator who prescribes that witness statements conform with the requirements of the Civil Procedure Rules, we are not aware of this being common practice. The form and content of witness statements can therefore vary.

In relation to the content of witness statements, although the purpose is to evidence facts within the knowledge of the witness, either because they witnessed an event themselves or were told something by someone else, we sometimes see witness statements used as a vehicle to set out a chronology of events by reference to documents. In the context of a time-limited procedure this is perhaps understandable, e.g. it may be that certain individuals with knowledge of the dispute or underlying project are tasked with pulling together the documentary evidence while others focus on the presentation of legal submissions and arguments. In and of itself this may be a time-efficient way of presenting a case, but it can be frustrating if the content of a witness statement is replicated in the head submission such that the adjudicator is required to read everything twice. In such circumstances it may be preferable for a separate chronology or catalogue of correspondence to be provided. It can be equally frustrating if a witness has included pages of general explanation on points not relevant to the dispute.

It may also be that, where the witness performed a function in their professional capacity, e.g. as a quantity surveyor, engineer or contract administrator, the witness statement explains how and why they have adopted a certain position. The witness statement may therefore include the witness's opinion, as a construction professional, on the valuation of work, its quality or the assessment of an entitlement to an extension of time. Although the function may be required to be undertaken in an independent manner, it cannot be said that such opinion evidence is truly independent in the same way as opinion evidence provided by an independent expert witness.

We are sometimes asked whether the fact a witness statement is accompanied by a statement of truth means that an adjudicator should afford it more weight. Although making a false statement to an adjudicator may affect the enforceability of the subsequent Decision (e.g. if the statement was found to have been made fraudulently and relied upon by the adjudicator), an adjudicator does not have the same powers as a judge or the ability to commit a lying witness for perjury. However, it may be that there is a subconscious positive effect on the adjudicator if a witness statement is signed and accompanied by a statement of truth. In our experience, though, where evidence contained in a witness statement is not accepted or is in dispute, the degree of weight to be placed upon such evidence will often depend on whether it is credible or consistent with a contemporaneously produced documentary record.

TYPES OF EVIDENCE: EXPERT EVIDENCE

Like witness statements, our experience in the United Kingdom and Ireland is that there is an increased prevalence of parties that rely on expert evidence in support of their cases in adjudication. We are aware that there is divergent opinion on whether expert evidence is appropriate in adjudication. Typical arguments against the use of experts are that the adjudicator may already possess the necessary expertise or that the adjudicator has the power to act inquisitorially, so they can conduct an investigation themselves. Although this may arguably be true, it should be remembered that adjudication is not expert determination, where the expert appointed to decide the dispute is normally entitled to use their own expertise.

Adjudicating a dispute requires the adjudicator to perform a quasi-judicial function. In performing that function, the adjudicator is under an obligation to comply with the rules of natural justice, part of which requires the adjudicator to allow the parties to advance their case and respond to the other side's case. The adjudicator is therefore required to decide the dispute that has been referred and argued in front of them and based on the evidence provided. As such, although it is permissible for an adjudicator to use their own expertise to evaluate and assess the submissions and evidence, it would not be permissible for the adjudicator to use their own private knowledge or expertise to determine the dispute without giving the parties the opportunity to comment. Further, in a time-limited procedure it may not be practicable for an adjudicator to conduct an investigation as an independent expert could, and then subsequently invite comment.

To a certain extent, the appropriateness of expert evidence will depend on the type of dispute that is referred to adjudication, and the types of dispute that may arise in connection with a construction project are very wide ranging. At a high level, we could categorize disputes according to whether they concern money, time or quality. However, those categories can be multifaceted, and many disputes will encompass issues relating to all three. Additionally, the size and complexity of the dispute referred may vary, as can the type of party or the experience of a party's representative. Alternatively, the dispute may be low in value. The short point to make is that adjudication is not a 'one size fits all' process, and it is therefore impossible to say, definitively, when expert evidence will be appropriate.

If we think of the types of dispute that may be referred to adjudication and the potential range of specialist technical and professional disciplines that may be involved in a construction project, it is not difficult to see why and how an adjudicator might be assisted by expert evidence in order to understand the dispute referred to them. Although adjudicators will be expected to have experience or knowledge of construction contracts and/or construction industry disputes, it is unlikely that one individual could be said to be an expert in all aspects of a construction contract or project. Even if the adjudicator has the required level of expertise, experience and/or qualification, in a claim against a professional for an alleged failure to exercise reasonable skill and care it is likely that a party making or defending a claim will seek (and arguably need) to rely on evidence from an independent expert of the same discipline as the professional in order to make out or defend the claim.

As for witness statements, to the best of our knowledge there are no prescribed procedural rules for expert evidence in adjudication. Again, we are aware of one UK adjudicator who requires experts to comply with the Civil Procedure Rules, but our experience is that that is an exception to the norm. Therefore, in contrast to the convention for arbitrators, who may include directions in their procedural orders for the rules that may apply to experts, the parties are likely to be left to their own devices in relation to how they seek to rely on and/or present expert evidence. This can give rise to difficulties as a result of a divergence of obligations imposed on experts depending on which professional body or organization they belong to (if any). For example, if an expert is a member of the RICS, they will be obliged to comply with the requirements of *Surveyors Acting as Expert Witnesses*,[1] a practice statement and guidance note from the RICS, and to support any evidence or report with a declaration. Members of expert accreditation bodies such as the Academy of Experts[2] or the Expert Witness Institute[3] will be required to provide similar declarations, and ultimately such experts may owe the same duty to an adjudicator as they would to a judge or arbitrator. Conversely, if an expert employed by the other side is not a member of such an organization, they might not be under the same duty or have the same obligations.

In our view there are three main distinguishing features that fall to be recognized in the context of the use of expert evidence in adjudication.

1 Royal Institute of Chartered Surveyors. 2014. *Surveyors Acting as Expert Witnesses*, 4th edition. RICS Practice Statement and Guidance Note, April (amended February 2023).

2 URL: https://academyofexperts.org/.

3 URL: https://www.ewi.org.uk/.

The first is the time constraints imposed by adjudication. These can affect the ability of an expert to conduct a full investigation, especially as the expert may not be in possession of all of the relevant documentation and/or the same documentation that the other side's expert is provided with. Although the limited extent of documentation may affect either side's expert, the time constraints can be particularly onerous for an expert who is instructed by a Responding Party, especially if that expert is instructed after the adjudication has commenced. As result of this, we sometimes find that expert reports or opinions are (understandably) heavily caveated.

The second feature, which we have already alluded to, is the potential for unequal obligations between experts who are not members of the same professional body or organization. Similarly, it may be that one party elects not to (or is unable to) instruct and/or declare that they have instructed an independent expert. For example, a party may elect to instruct an 'expert' to act partially, i.e. effectively as a 'hired gun', with the objective of attacking or discrediting the opinion or evidence of the independent expert instructed by the other side.

The final feature (and one that arguably applies to all evidence in adjudication) is that the nature of adjudication is such that the expert evidence is likely to be subjected to a lesser degree of scrutiny than it would be in litigation or arbitration involving cross-examination. This is due to the limited time available for the parties and the adjudicator to assess the evidence, as well as the fact that there is unlikely to be a formal hearing involving cross-examination. In our experience, this feature can affect the quality of the expert evidence due to the fact that the adjudication is likely to be restricted to the parties and their respective teams, such that the proceedings will be conducted in private and the Decision will therefore have a limited audience. In contrast, in litigation, the proceedings may be conducted in public and the judgment is likely to be available to the public, such that any poor behaviour on the part of the expert can be the subject of judicial comment. The expert may therefore be less accountable and/or can sometimes be tempted to veer more towards the approach of a 'hired gun'. The adjudicator should be alive to this possibility and account for the risk that an expert may not be acting in a truly independent manner.

We have experienced a wide range of types of expert in the course of our adjudication practice, as follows.

(i) Technical experts:

  (a) engineering, e.g. structural, civil, geotechnical, mechanical and electrical services, etc.;
  (b) architectural, e.g. general, cladding, planning, etc.;
  (c) building, e.g. defects, construction methods, etc.;
  (d) fire safety/building regulations;
  (e) IT/computing;
  (f) handwriting; and
  (g) meteorological.

(ii) Delay/programming experts.

(iii) Quantum experts:

  (a) quantity surveying/construction costs;
  (b) accountancy; and
  (c) property valuation.

The experts that we see most commonly are probably quantity surveyors and delay analysts.

We sometimes get asked whether the involvement of experts is helpful to us as adjudicators. In answering that question, it is instructive to consider what the purpose of expert evidence is, and this will depend on whether you are considering it from the perspective of the parties or of the adjudicator.

From the parties' perspective, they may be looking for an expert to provide a truly independent opinion in order to decide on strategy or to identify strengths and weaknesses in their case. Additionally, assuming the objective is to win, they will be looking for an expert to assist their case or undermine the other side's case (particularly if responding). In contrast, the adjudicator will be looking to the experts to assist their understanding of the disputes and issues between the parties, to increase the efficiency of the process, and to make their job easier. Therefore, to the extent an expert assists in achieving this purpose, it can be said that the involvement of experts might be useful.

However, it is worth again stating that the quality of experts can vary. A good expert can both assist an adjudicator in reconciling the differences between the parties (or their experts) and help to identify and distil the issues that might require determination, e.g. providing confirmation of what is agreed and what is not agreed. If time permits, providing an opinion on either side's case can be helpful, particularly on quantum or delay. Finally, an expert restricting their opinion to matters that fall within their expertise is not only helpful to the adjudicator, but arguably it will also assist their client as their credibility will be maintained.

In contrast, an expert who is obviously partisan, overly enthusiastic about their client's case and considers themselves as an advocate for their client is obviously a bad one, and they are likely to do more harm than good. Further irritants are reports from opposing experts that read like 'ships passing in the night', i.e. ones that do not opine on or respond to the opposing expert's opinion or report, and opinions in a report that sit on the fence and effectively say nothing. Finally, experts should steer clear of providing opinions on issues of liability: that is the domain of the party representative(s) and also something that the adjudicator is ultimately charged with deciding.

Although we both have experience of bad experts, our experience has, in the main, been positive, particularly where experts have been involved in adjudications concerning high-value or complex disputes. We also believe that good adjudicators will be alive to the time constraints and the potential for imbalance between experts instructed by the Referring and Responding Parties, such that the fact that an expert's report is not as extensive as might have been ideal should not necessarily have an adverse effect.

DEALING WITH REQUESTS FOR DOCUMENTS

Although there is no formal system of 'disclosure' or 'discovery' in adjudication, the adjudicator will invariably have the power to request or order documents to be provided. For example, pursuant to paragraph 13(1) of Part I of the Scheme, an adjudicator has the power to 'request any party to the contract to supply him with such documents as he may reasonably require including, if he so directs, any written statement from any party to the contract supporting or supplementing the referral notice and any other documents given under paragraph 7(2)'. This may be done of the adjudicator's own volition, or at the request of a party. If it is a simple or non-contentious request, it may be appropriate for the adjudicator to simply ask for the document to be provided without inviting comment. Such a request may be for a document to be produced in its native format, e.g. a spreadsheet or a programme file. However, if the request is more wide ranging or does not appear to be straightforward, it may be appropriate to first ask whether the party who has been asked to provide the documents is in a position to provide them and, if so, when it would be able to do so. Again, if there is no resistance to the documents being provided, then it is a simple matter of confirming this.

In circumstances where the request is resisted, we would typically ask the party making the request to explain why the documents are relevant and ask the other party to explain why it does not consider the request should be granted. Although each case will be dependent on the facts, to the extent the adjudicator forms the view that the documents are relevant and that they can be provided in relatively short order, then we see no reason why the documents should not be provided. Conversely, if the relevance is not understood and/or the documents cannot be easily accessed or provided, e.g. because they are not within that party's control and/or to do so would breach some form of confidentiality, it may be appropriate to decline the request.

If the absence and/or late provision of documents adversely impacts on a party's ability to prepare a submission, it may also be necessary to adjust the timetable.

DEALING WITH 'WITHOUT PREJUDICE' OR 'PRIVILEGED' MATERIAL

Although it is not common, we sometimes find that documents marked 'without prejudice' or 'privileged' are included in the supporting documents. Although the mere fact that a document is marked as such may not necessarily mean that it is actually 'without prejudice' or 'privileged', if such documents are discovered by the adjudicator we consider it prudent to write to the parties to inform them of the discovery and invite comment. We would also record whether or not we had read the content of the document, although it is likely that we would stop reading the document as soon as we saw that it was marked as without prejudice or privileged. If the parties agree that the document should be removed, then it can be deleted from the electronic file and/or removed from the hard copy file and securely disposed of, with the adjudicator recording their actions both at the time and, in due course, in the Decision.

We also find that parties sometimes claim that certain documents or references to discussions should not have been included on the grounds that they were without prejudice or privileged. Again, if the parties accept that they are and that they should be removed – and so long as the document or references have not already been read – that will be the end of the matter. However, if the documents have been read and/or the parties do not agree that the documents are indeed without prejudice or privileged, the adjudicator will need to determine whether the documents actually are without prejudice or privileged. If the conclusion is that they are and they have been read, the adjudicator will need to consider whether the fact that they have been read will unduly affect their ability to act in a procedurally fair manner.

When we have faced this type of situation in the past, we have asked the parties whether they would object to a suitably qualified colleague examining the documents in question in order to reach a conclusion as to whether they are truly without prejudice or privileged. Assuming there is no objection to this, then if the colleague concludes that the documents are subject to privilege and should not have been disclosed, we would arrange for them to be removed. Conversely, if the conclusion is that the documents are not privileged, we would confirm that to the parties, albeit we would then still probably undertake our own check just to satisfy ourselves that our colleague's conclusion was correct.

The fact that an adjudicator has read a document or references to discussions that were privileged or without prejudice will not, in itself, always result in a finding that the adjudicator was unduly affected by, or perceived to be biased on account of, having read the document or references. While it will depend on the jurisdiction, the key question is normally whether, objectively viewed, the adjudicator is able to put such knowledge out of their mind such that it would not affect their findings in relation to the substantive dispute or issues. For example, the fact that an offer might have been made could be viewed as being a wholly commercial decision, and as such it should not influence an adjudicator's decision on liability; after all, an adjudicator will appreciate that settlement discussions and offers are commonplace in commercial disputes. However, that may not be the case if liability was being hotly contested by a party and a without prejudice or privileged document confirmed that that party had accepted liability and only challenged quantum. In the event the adjudicator concluded that they could not (or that there was a risk that they could not) reach a decision on a substantive issue with a clear mind, then the appropriate course of action would be to resign.

DEALING WITH REQUESTS FOR FURTHER SUBMISSIONS AND UNSOLICITED SUBMISSIONS

Having set directions and a procedure with a prescribed number of submissions, it is not uncommon to receive requests for further submissions. If the request is straightforward and there is sufficient time to accommodate it within the existing timetable without affecting the Decision date, then a simple confirmation of consent can be made. If a further submission could affect the Decision date, though, we would invite comments from the other side.

Where a request is contested, we would seek clarification from the party seeking permission as to why they wish to make a further submission, including which aspects, or even specific paragraphs, of the preceding document it wishes to address if applicable. We would also seek clarification of when it anticipates being in a position to make the submission if permitted to do so.

If the adjudicator is on top of the submissions and is sufficiently appraised of the dispute, they should be able to form a view about whether a further submission on the matter identified is relevant and/or necessary. If the adjudicator knows that the party making the application has already established its position on that matter, then it is easy for the adjudicator to disallow the request. However, if the matter is material and either unresolved or the adjudicator is uncertain of the outcome, it may be prudent to allow the submission and then address any consequential effect on the timetable. One way of addressing adjustments to the timetable is to allow the submission only if the party making the request extends time and also allows the other party the opportunity to comment (in the event the adjudicator considers it necessary). If the power to extend time is within the sole gift of the party making the application, then it may be relatively straightforward to obtain consent. However, where the consent of both parties is required, this will require managing, with the adjudicator's persuasive case-management skills coming to the fore. It might therefore be prudent to make consent subject to certain conditions that the other party could find acceptable.

The adjudicator may also want to impose a page limit for the narrative of a further submission, including any associated factual and/or expert evidence, or to simply make clear that they do not anticipate the submission needing to exceed a certain number of pages. Experience has taught us that it is prudent to make clear that the further submission must have the same page size and the same paragraph and font formatting as previous submissions. This avoids a party changing the page margins, paragraph spacing and/or font size to accommodate their further submission within the defined page limit!

Even where we set directions that prior permission should be sought for further submissions beyond those that we originally directed the parties could serve, we still find that some parties will make unsolicited submissions. This is less than ideal, especially when we have started working on the Decision on the assumption that submissions have closed. For this reason we consider it good practice for the adjudicator to confirm to the parties when the point comes that they do not require any further submission and that they are proceeding to prepare their Decision. That said, this will not necessarily prevent a party making an uninvited submission.

Although unsolicited submissions may be unwelcome, it is perhaps understandable why a party or their representative will consider it in their interests to make them. Indeed, there may be good reason: for example, a new point might come to light, or some new evidence that is considered to be material might be uncovered. Therefore, despite the fact that permission not being sought can be irritating, our view is that a measured approach is required here. The question is one of whether the submission should or should not be admitted.

When dealing with unsolicited submissions, similar principles to those that apply for requests for further submissions will apply regarding relevance and the impact on the timetable. So, if the new submission is deemed necessary and if there is sufficient time to admit it and facilitate any necessary further comment, there may be no need to disallow it. Similarly, if adjustment to the timetable is needed, this will need to be sought and obtained. If permission to extend is not given, it might be appropriate for the adjudicator to make the point that they might not be able to fully take the submission into account and/or that they would take into account the lateness of the submission, its unsolicited nature and the fact that the other party might not have the opportunity to respond in detail.

Finally, it may be the case that while neither party seeks to make further submissions, the adjudicator considers that particular submissions would be of assistance to them in deciding the dispute: relating to specific aspects of the preceding submissions, for example. The adjudicator should therefore ask for the further submissions, which could be in the form of written narratives or emails in answer to questions posed by the adjudicator to one or both parties. In our experience, such further submissions can be helpful, although we consider it to be sensible for adjudicators to collate questions for the parties into a small number of emails rather than bombarding them with too many messages whenever the adjudicator has a question. That can lead to confusion.

CHAPTER 6

Meetings and site inspections

The extent to which an adjudicator elects to convene a meeting or site inspection will vary between different adjudicators and jurisdictions. It may also depend on the nature of the dispute that has been referred, the quality of the submissions and the extent to which the supporting documents have been properly organized and indexed, and also the ability of the parties' representatives. We are aware that there are some adjudicators who do not consider that meetings are appropriate at all and who consider that all adjudications should be conducted on a documents-only basis. While we do not subscribe to that school of thought, it is fair to say that there is a difference between the two of us in relation to the frequency at which we convene meetings. We are also aware that in Australia, and in other jurisdictions that adopt the 'narrow' dispute model, adjudications meetings are almost unheard of.

We recall that when adjudication was being introduced in Ireland there was much talk about the fact that it was a constitutional right for a party to have an oral hearing and for proceedings to be conducted in Irish. This led some to believe that an adjudicator would be obliged to convene an oral hearing, but the Irish High Court has since provided clarification that an adjudicator is free to conduct an adjudication on a documents-only basis without necessarily offending a party's right to a fair hearing.

RELEVANT CASE LAW

In the Irish case of *John Paul Construction Limited v Tipperary Co-Operative Creamery Limited,*[1] Mr Justice Garrett Simons stated at paragraph 13:

1 [2022] IEHC 3.

'In the present case, the principal ground advanced for resisting enforcement involves an allegation that the adjudicator failed to consider the defence put forward to the claim by the paying party. Were this allegation to be made out on the facts, then it would justify the refusal of leave to enforce the adjudicator's decision. Making all due allowance for the provisional nature of an adjudicator's decision, and for the exigencies of the expedited procedure mandated under the legislation, fair procedures nevertheless demand that a party be afforded a right to be heard before a decision is reached requiring that party to make a payment under a construction contract. A right to be heard implies a right to have one's submissions considered by the decision-maker. The right to be heard does not necessarily, however, extend to a right to an oral hearing: having regard to the summary and expeditious nature of statutory adjudication, it will be rare, if ever, that an adjudicator is required to convene an oral hearing.'

FACTORS IN DECIDING WHETHER TO HOLD A MEETING OR UNDERTAKE A SITE INSPECTION

The first time the prospect of a meeting being convened might arise is when one is setting the initial procedural directions and timetable. The types of meeting required in adjudication generally fall into two distinct categories: the first is a meeting to address any initial timetabling or procedural issues; and the second is a meeting in relation to the underlying substantive dispute.

We sometimes find that initial scheduling issues result in extensive correspondence between the parties as to what timetable is reasonable. Additionally, the competing positions of the parties may be poles apart: for example, one party might contend that it has a right to have the dispute determined within the minimum period prescribed in the contract or statute while the other party says it needs weeks or months just to be able to put its response. Although it may be possible to resolve the timetable by written correspondence, it may actually be preferable – and more cost and time effective – for the adjudicator to call a procedural meeting with the parties' representatives to address the timetable question. This is especially true if the meeting can be convened via an online meeting platform.

As well as reducing or potentially putting an end to the endless exchanges of email correspondence, getting the parties together in a meeting can sometimes encourage a more outwardly collaborative or reasonable approach by the parties. Although some parties may have positively elected to adopt 'guerilla'-type or aggressive tactics, with a target placed not only on the other party but also on the adjudicator, most parties will wish to be seen as reasonable by the adjudicator. We therefore sometimes find that the 'keyboard-warrior' types present as more reasonable or 'soften' when they meet in person (or at least when they are seen online). We also find that the adjudicator can use their soft skills to persuade parties to agree to a timetable, either as a result of shared thoughts or by way of compromise. We therefore find that convening a short procedural meeting can sometimes result in an agreed timetable. Even when an agreed timetable cannot be achieved at such a meeting, the information exchanged or discussed at the meeting may enable the adjudicator to reach a more informed view as to what constitutes a reasonable timetable, taking into account the nature and extent of the dispute referred, the availability of relevant individuals and the requirement to comply with the rules of natural justice.

Turning to the question of whether to hold a meeting to address the underlying substantive dispute, if it is obvious that the adjudication can be conducted on a documents-only basis, then it is a straightforward matter of issuing directions and confirming that the matter will be conducted based on the written submissions and documentary evidence. For example, if the dispute is about whether or not a notice was sent either on time or at all, this might be something that lends itself to a documents-only procedure. Similarly, matters of legal interpretation may be suited to being determined on the basis of documentary submissions.

Where the position is not so clear, we may either canvass the parties' views as to whether a meeting is deemed necessary or, alternatively, provide for a meeting on a provisional basis pending receipt of any responsive submissions. The same approach can apply to the question of whether a site inspection is necessary. The rationale for making provisional arrangements is to restrict the potential for delay at a later date as a result of diaries being filled. Setting a date at an earlier stage enables the relevant personnel to hold an appointment in their diaries and/or enables any availability issues to be accounted for when setting the initial timetable.

We would stress that, even when the parties are canvassed for their views as to whether a meeting or site inspection is necessary, the ultimate decision is the adjudicator's. That said, if both parties are agreed that a meeting or site inspection would be beneficial, this may be a significant factor in the adjudicator's decision. In such circumstances, we consider it more likely than not that we would convene a meeting.

Where there is a possibility of a meeting and a provisional date has been set, we tend to defer the decision on its necessity until after the Response has been served. We consider it important to communicate the decision on whether a meeting is to be convened as soon as possible. In order to reach a conclusion and decide whether to convene a meeting, the adjudicator will need to be on top of the submissions and be familiar with the documents that have been provided. Thus, by the time the Response has been served, the content of the Referral should have been reviewed such that it does not delay the review of the Response and the supporting documentation when they are served. Once the Response is served, we would send an initial acknowledgement and advise that we would revert to the parties regarding the necessity for a meeting once the submission has been considered.

The first question we ask ourselves when considering whether a meeting or site inspection is needed is whether it is possible to reach a Decision without one. If the submissions are clear, the supporting documentation is well referenced and accessible, the competing positions are well articulated and the issues are identifiable, a meeting might well be unnecessary. Conversely, if there was no such clarity and the adjudicator was unclear as to the issues to be determined, or if the parties' position on a point (or points) or the relevance of the supporting documents were not understood, it may be that a meeting is necessary to assist the adjudicator's understanding of the dispute and the issues to be determined.

The next question we would ask is whether a meeting is desirable, and in making that assessment we would consider the costs involved. A related question is whether convening a meeting is likely to involve the adjudicator spending more or less time on the matter. However, the adjudicator's fees are only one aspect of the costs question because, although a meeting may result in a reduction in the number of hours spent by the adjudicator, e.g. reducing the amount of time reading potentially irrelevant documents, incomprehensible submissions or repetitive witness statements, the costs to the parties of preparing for and attending a meeting may be significant. In some cases, such additional expense may be justified or proportionate to the sums in issue or the importance of the dispute to the parties, but this might not always be the case. An additional day spent by the adjudicator in rereading or reviewing the documents in more detail could therefore result in an overall reduction in the costs of the adjudication. Furthermore, setting out queries or requests for clarification in writing might be more cost and time effective, particularly as such queries may only arise once the adjudicator gets into the detail of the submissions and is reaching findings on each issue. The increase in the parties' costs can sometimes be lost on adjudicators as a result of the fact that not all adjudicators have experience of either representing parties or of dealing with the parties' costs. It can therefore be helpful to consider the hourly cost of the individuals who may be required to attend a meeting. If the meeting is likely to be attended by lawyers or claims consultants, experts and senior staff, the cost of a short meeting could far outweigh any increase in the adjudicator's fees.

As well as cost, we then need to consider whether a meeting or site inspection is necessary in order for justice to be 'seen to be done'. To a certain extent, this is a question of self-protection for the adjudicator. The chances are that at least one of the parties may be aggrieved with the Decision and may on occasion seek to contend that the process was procedurally unfair because the adjudicator did not conduct a meeting or inspect the site in order to allow that party to present their case. This may be in the form of an argument before a judge in enforcement proceedings or as a complaint to an ANA/ANB or to the adjudicator's professional body. Paradoxically, the fact that an adjudicator elected to convene a meeting or site inspection may also result in a complaint, especially if a party felt ambushed as a result of new arguments or submissions presented at a meeting. This can be a case of being damned if you do, dammed if you don't! Nevertheless, it is useful to consider the necessity for a meeting from the perspective of the potential losing party.

In deciding whether to convene a meeting, it may be that the scope of the meeting can be limited to certain discrete points that the adjudicator requires assistance with. This can also impact on the costs question. For example, it may be that the meeting is restricted to legal, technical, programming or quantum issues (or a combination thereof). When addressing technical, programming or quantum issues, it may be that there is no need for the party representatives or lawyers to attend, and this could result in a cost saving. Alternatively, it may be that the meeting could be timetabled in such a way that only part attendance was required.

Turning to the question of site inspections, we find that the purpose of these can be twofold. First, they might enable the adjudicator to familiarize themselves with the project or the site. This can sometimes help to put the submissions and evidence in context. Second, they allow the adjudicator to inspect work that is alleged to be defective. Obviously, if the alleged defective work had been remedied, there may be little benefit in such an inspection. Where it is not obvious from the submissions or evidence provided whether the alleged defects have been remedied, this may require the question to be asked. Where no such remedial work has been undertaken, it is likely that an inspection may assist. Again, from the perspective of a potential losing party, the failure of an adjudicator to inspect work that was alleged to be defective may give rise to a complaint, especially if there were no legal issues that might alleviate responsibility for the alleged defect.

ONLINE VERSUS IN PERSON

Allied to the question of the cost of convening a meeting or site inspection is whether it is held via an online meeting platform, in person or a combination of both (i.e. a hybrid), with some attending in person and others dialling-in online. Having decided that a meeting is necessary, we would, in the first instance, canvass the parties' views regarding the appropriate forum as well as the location or venue in the event it is considered that an in-person meeting is appropriate. If the parties agree, or one party expresses no preference, making the appropriate arrangements should be easy. In contrast, if there are competing views, the parties' differences will need to be resolved and a decision made.

The location of any meeting and the number of each party's attendees will be key considerations in deciding whether to hold a meeting online or in person. Again, the costs of the adjudicator travelling to a location for an in-person meeting may be far less than the costs of the parties attending a meeting in that location. Also, the means of transport for the adjudicator and the extent to which time spent travelling could usefully be spent working on the documents (such that it did not represent pure 'travel time') may be a relevant consideration. That is, travelling by train, plane or taxi may enable an adjudicator to work on the file and result in a corresponding reduction in the overall time taken.

Also, the cost of providing a venue and catering may be a factor to consider. If one party is willing to host, and no objection is made, then the costs may not be an issue. However, if neutrality and/or a venue that is roughly equidistant between the parties is required, those costs might need to be taken into account. To address neutrality, it may be that the adjudicator has the ability to host a meeting at no cost to the parties. That may not be possible, though, in which case a hired venue might be needed. When a chargeable venue is chosen, we will sometimes ask the parties whether they wish for the costs to be treated as an adjudicator's expense. However, in such circumstances we would still ask either one or both of the parties to attend to booking and payment in the first instance, but to advise us of the costs so we could account for them in our Decision.

Once a cost assessment is undertaken, the question then arises of whether the additional costs of convening a meeting in person are justifiable in the context of the size and importance of the dispute to the parties. Again, the greater the sum in the dispute and the greater the amount of time and cost the parties have invested in the adjudication, the easier it is to justify additional expense.

Another key consideration is procedural fairness. This could arise in the context of whether the costs incurred by one party may be disproportionately higher than for the other party, e.g. because of their location. This could also arise in the context of choice of venue: is a neutral venue desirable in terms of the perception of fairness? In such circumstances, convening the meeting online may provide a solution that is not only cost effective but also procedurally fair.

It is fair to say that, prior to the Covid-19 pandemic, convening an online meeting to address the substantive issues was unusual. This changed during the lockdowns, especially where in-person meetings were not permitted. Consequently, parties (and adjudicators) became more familiar with and capable of conducting online meetings. Indeed, some think that the ability for attendees to share their screens, so that everyone is looking at the same documents at the same time, actually makes for a better or more effective way of conducting a meeting, especially where the documents have been provided electronically.

A further advantage of online meetings is the ease with which they can be recorded, including with a timestamp. We would therefore suggest that, unless the parties agree or there is no material cost difference to conducting a meeting in person, there is no reason for meetings not to be conducted online.

Although the question of an online or in-person forum mainly arises in respect of meetings with the parties, it can also arise in relation to site inspections. For example, it may be possible to conduct a site inspection via a video stream or drone footage, either live or via a recording. Again, this can be a cost-effective means of inspecting a site or alleged defective workmanship, especially if the site or project is some distance away and/or there are restrictions on obtaining access.

WHO SHOULD ATTEND?

The question of who should attend a meeting or site inspection will depend on its purpose. The adjudicator may expressly specify that they wish for certain individuals to attend: certain factual witnesses or team members, for example, or the authors of expert reports or individuals who are familiar with the project or subject matter. Alternatively, the adjudicator may leave the attendees to the parties' discretion. If that is the case, the parties will need to know what the purpose of the meeting is in order to determine who should attend.

When we leave the identity of the attendees to the parties' discretion, we always ask the parties to tell us the names of their proposed attendees some days in advance of the meeting or site inspection. This is for a number of reasons. From a practical perspective, the venue will need to be able to accommodate the number of attendees, or there may be a requirement for prior notification or security clearance. Furthermore, if the meeting is online, meeting invitations will need to be sent. Also, it is only fair that the parties know who is attending from the other side to help them decide who should attend on their behalf.

Even if there are no logistical restrictions, there might still be objections from a party regarding the number and/or appropriateness of attendees that the other party wished to bring to a meeting or site inspection. A decision will then need to be made by the adjudicator concerning said attendees. A key consideration should be whether attendance is required to assist the adjudicator. Other key considerations are questions regarding procedural fairness and associated costs. So, if one party wished for its lawyer to attend a meeting that was not addressing any legal issues, the adjudicator might be justified in excluding lawyers from said meeting. Likewise, a meeting to address purely technical issues could be restricted either to the individuals who had direct knowledge of the issues or to those who had provided technical expert reports; and a meeting in an adjudication concerning a valuation dispute could be restricted to the quantity surveyors who had prepared the competing valuations.

Where both a site inspection and a meeting with the parties is deemed necessary, it may be that those who attend each differs, even if they are convened on the same day. If the purpose of the site inspection is familiarization, then it may be that there is a limited invitation list for the site inspection – perhaps just one or two individuals from each side (equal numbers to demonstrate fairness or parity) – with a greater list of attendees at the meeting. Similarly, it may be that some attendees only need to attend the part of a meeting that is relevant to them. This is one reason why an agenda and an outline timetable will be helpful to the parties, as we discuss below.

PREPARING FOR A MEETING OR SITE VISIT

As well as advising the parties of the purpose of the meeting, it may also be helpful for an adjudicator to advise them of the procedure they intend to adopt. For example, does the adjudicator require oral submissions and/or explanations on any point? Will the adjudicator expect or allow the parties to question factual witnesses or experts, or will they wish to conduct the questioning themselves? Ordinarily, the approach we would adopt is to question the witnesses and/or experts ourselves, but if the parties have engaged experienced specialist counsel and/or the dispute concerns allegations of professional negligence and/or involves experts with diametrically opposed opinions, some form of cross-examination might be deemed appropriate, especially if the sums in dispute are significant.

We also advocate an agenda and estimated timeline being provided by the adjudicator. As well as informing the parties of the matters that the adjudicator wishes to cover – which helps the parties decide who is best placed to attend and aids in their preparation for the meeting – it should help the adjudicator both prepare for the meeting and manage it on the day. An agenda and timeline can also help an adjudicator decide whether or not it is possible to fit the meeting into one day. Even if it possible to hold a meeting in one day, it might be sensible to split the meeting across two days on account of availability issues or because it is otherwise convenient to do so, e.g. one meeting could focus on legal or delay-related issues and another could focus on quantum. Again, the attendees could differ between days.

EXAMPLE 6.1: SAMPLE MEETING AGENDA

Party A v Party B – Adjudication Meeting Agenda

Meeting date: 19 December 2023
Meeting venue: Party A's offices

1. **09.00** Introductions and house-keeping
2. **09:15** Delay:
   - Baseline programme
   - Windows 1 to 9
3. **10:45** Refreshment break
4. **11:00** Delay:
   - Windows 1 to 9 (continued)
5. **12:30** Lunch
6. **13:15** Quantum:
   - Non-direct costs
     - Prolongation and preliminaries thickening
     - Acceleration
     - Site-wide operational costs
7. **14:45** Refreshment break
8. **15:00** Quantum:
   - Non-direct costs (continued)
   - Direct costs
9. **17:00** Any other business

In advance of the meeting, the adjudicator should familiarize themselves with the submissions and supporting documents. To a certain extent, it is likely that an adjudicator will have to do that in order to reach a decision as to whether a meeting is deemed necessary in the first place. In so doing, the adjudicator should note any points that might require clarification, as well as any questions they might wish to put to the parties' representatives, factual witnesses or experts. As well as assisting them in the formulation of the agenda, doing this will enable the adjudicator to determine who may be best placed to attend and also which questions to ask. Some adjudicators might wish to prepare a detailed list of questions, while others might prefer to make a mental note or jot down a shorthand or abbreviated prompt. Ultimately, the approach adopted will depend on what works best for the individual adjudicator. The most important point is that the adjudicator is well prepared, thereby instilling confidence in the parties that they understand the issues in dispute. The meeting is not the place for an adjudicator to learn about the dispute for the first time. That said, it may be that one of the reasons for calling the meeting is that the adjudicator is unable to understand the issues or extent of the dispute from the submissions and documents provided.

In relation to online meetings, if the task of setting up the meeting and issuing invitations to the preferred email addresses of the named attendees has not been delegated to one of the parties, the adjudicator will need to do this. In order to do so, the parties will obviously have needed to provide the relevant information. Another factor to consider is whether the online meeting is to be recorded. If so, it would be sensible to advise the parties in advance. Although this is more pertinent to online meetings, the same considerations may also apply to recording of in-person meetings. It is not something that we tend to do, but we do know of adjudicators who use specialist recording software on their laptops.

When preparing for a site inspection (or even a meeting that is being conducted on site), the adjudicator will need to determine exactly where they are going to meet the parties. This is particularly important on large sites with a number of entrances. It may also be sensible for the adjudicator to ask whether they need to make arrangements for their own personal protective equipment (PPE) in advance. Typically, we find that arrangements for PPE will be made by the parties (although it may involve the disclosure of the adjudicator's shoe size!), but if not, the adjudicator will need to ensure they have suitable PPE to avoid any embarrassment or wasted expense on the day. On a related point, it may be that access is conditional on attendance at an induction or on security clearance or identification checks. Again, it may be sensible for the adjudicator to seek confirmation in advance so that arrangements can be made.

ON THE DAY

There will be practical points for the adjudicator to consider: how to get to the venue on the day, for example, and how long it is likely to take. Any delays encountered on the day or any connectivity issues if the meeting is online will need to be communicated to the parties. We would also recommend that the adjudicator has a backup device available for online meetings, just in case any hardware issues arise on the day. The main considerations we address in the remainder of this chapter, however, relate to the conduct of the meeting or site inspection itself.

While the parties (or, perhaps more likely, their representatives) may have encountered the adjudicator before, this is certainly not always the case. The meeting or site inspection may consequently be the first time, and sometimes the only time, that the adjudicator is seen or met by the parties, their representatives and other attendees. This is therefore the opportunity for the adjudicator to demonstrate they are familiar with the dispute, that they are well prepared, and that they have the ability to manage and control a meeting or site inspection. Being unprepared or allowing the meeting or site inspection to descend into chaos will not instil confidence in the parties.

In our view, it is important for the adjudicator to set the right tone. That does not mean an adjudicator should be overly authoritarian, but we do consider that a degree of formality and control is required. The adjudicator should therefore act as the chair of the meeting and should also display neutrality in the way they conduct themselves towards the parties, their representatives and the case. Being overly familiar with one party (or their representative) on account of a previous acquaintance would therefore be inappropriate, especially if the other party or representative is unknown to the adjudicator.

Although it sounds an obvious point, the adjudicator should avoid being placed in a situation where they are in the presence of a representative of one party without a representative from the other party also being present. This is easier to control if the meeting is being conducted online, as attendees can be admitted at the same time, but even then it might be that an attendee has connectivity issues. This may be a good reason for the meeting to be recorded, so that a party can at least have access to the recording after the event to avoid any suggestion that the adjudicator had any unilateral conversations that the other party did not have the opportunity of commenting on.

In-person meetings or site inspections can increase the possibility of an adjudicator being placed in a situation where they are alone with one party, e.g. in a lift, in a reception area, or in the meeting room when one party has retired. The adjudicator will therefore need to be alive to the situation and, if possible, avoid it or remove themselves from it if it happens. If this is not possible, it may be sensible to explain to the party who is present that it is not appropriate for them or you to discuss the case and thereafter to explain the circumstances to the other party at the first opportunity to avoid any suggestions of impropriety at a later date. Adjudicators should keep in mind the possibility that at least one party may be aggrieved by their eventual Decision!

We always start meetings with introductions, taking care to note down names and roles. If the meeting is online, this provides an opportunity to test connections and sound, etc. Thereafter, we proceed through the agenda, keeping an eye on timings. We also take care to keep notes of meetings, including any action points. Even if the meeting is being recorded, it is useful for the adjudicator to make contemporaneous notes of their thoughts and to record any observations on what has been seen or heard. This is not for the purpose of producing a record or minutes (we would not recommend doing so in any event), but to assist in the preparation of the Decision.

Keeping control of the meeting and the parties, in terms of both timing and behaviour, can sometimes be a challenge. It may therefore be sensible to set out some ground rules at the outset, e.g. asking participants not to interrupt each other. Even then, tempers may be running high and it may be necessary to intervene and be more assertive in order to call order. This is not to say that a witness or expert displaying anger is always unhelpful (perhaps less so for their party!), especially if the adjudicator is required to assess a witness's evidence or an expert's opinion. In some instances, it might be necessary to take a break in order to allow things to cool a little or to speak to the representatives themselves (together) to ask them to control their clients.

Another situation we sometime see is an argument being made, or evidence being produced, for the first time at a meeting. The adjudicator may then be faced with an objection or a request to respond. If the matter can be addressed on the day, perhaps with the benefit of a short break, then that might be the most efficient way of addressing the issue. However, if that is not possible, further directions might be required so as to afford a party the opportunity to address the new argument or evidence in writing after the meeting or site inspection.

We invariably include an 'any other business' item on our agenda. The purpose of this is threefold: for the adjudicator to ask the parties whether they wish to raise any matter (either arising from the meeting or otherwise); for the adjudicator to raise any matters not included on the agenda; and also to confirm any agreed action points. If there are no further submissions to follow, this might also be the moment to confirm the date when the adjudicator expects to publish their Decision. On a related note, it might also be the case that the meeting provides the opportunity to seek the parties' agreement for more time in the event it becomes evident that it is needed, perhaps on account of matters arising from the meeting. Again, it might be easier to obtain the parties' agreement in person than it is via correspondence.

CHAPTER 7

Dealing with different types of party and dispute

We have already identified the variety of disputes that may arise under or in connection with construction contracts. As well as a wide variation in the types of dispute that may be referred to adjudication, the type of party and the behaviour of the parties or representatives can also vary. Consequently, a one-size-fits-all approach does not apply. What is appropriate for a large complex dispute with sophisticated representatives may not be appropriate for a dispute between a 'jobbing' builder and a homeowner who are both unrepresented. In this chapter we share our thoughts regarding some of the features of the different type of party and dispute that can be encountered and the approach that might be appropriate in order to deal with the different situations an adjudicator may be faced with.

PARTIES AND REPRESENTATIVES

Aggressive

Whether they set out intending to be or otherwise, we sometimes encounter aggressive parties or party representatives. As well as being directed at the opposing party, the aggression can sometimes be targeted at the adjudicator – or at least it can feel like that! To a certain extent this type of behaviour or conduct may be understandable, particularly from the parties themselves. Being involved in a formal dispute resolution process that is unfamiliar can be stressful. Furthermore, the consequences of an adverse Decision can be significant and could result in insolvency, job losses or other personal difficulties.

Although a good advocate or representative will not allow themselves to become personally attached to a client's case, those who advance or defend claims will have a 'litigation mindset' and they will want to win. They may also have an interest in the outcome of the case, either in terms of a continued relationship with their client, a financial incentive (such as a success-related fee arrangement) or just as a result of pure competitiveness! They may therefore be heavily invested in the dispute. Party representatives may also be under pressure from their clients to be aggressive, but we would add that we see certain representatives adopt an aggressive stance as a matter of course – something that might simply be a product of human nature.

In our view, when an adjudicator is faced with an aggressive party or representative it is important for them to remain neutral and not 'enter the arena'. This can be difficult, especially in the electronic communications era when there can be a tendency to reply and press send without fully reflecting on how the reply may be viewed at a later date. Although a judge or investigating body who is asked to consider an adjudicator's conduct may be sympathetic to an adjudicator who has been provoked by an aggressive approach, that may not always be the case. We would therefore encourage adjudicators to take their time and to think about how a reply may come across later before sending it. Sometimes, leaving the email in a draft folder and, if possible, deferring it until after a good night's sleep, or until the next working day if drafting at the weekend, may result in a more temperate and measured response.

As well as leaving some time before sending a reply, we consider it helpful to depersonalize from any aggressive correspondence that is received. Although the correspondence may be unwelcome and perceived as a personal attack, it may just be misdirected and not intended as such. The adjudicator might simply have been caught in the crossfire. It is therefore helpful if an adjudicator can develop a thick skin when faced with such correspondence.

Homeowners, residential owner-occupiers and unrepresented parties

Although we have grouped homeowners and residential owner-occupiers with unrepresented parties, these categories are not always synonymous. We have used this grouping because, in our experience, these types of party may not always be familiar with the adjudication process, but, again, this is a generalism and we have certainly encountered parties who fall into these categories who have considerable experience of the process. For present purposes, though, we shall assume that this category of party is not familiar with the adjudication process.

Although construction contracts involving homeowners and residential owner-occupiers are not subject to statutory adjudication in certain jurisdictions, some homeowners and residential owner-occupiers nevertheless agree that their contracts will provide for disputes to be referred to adjudication. We are also aware that there are some specific homeowner adjudication provisions that allow these parties to refer disputes to adjudication. Although these provisions may allow the adjudicator to act in an 'expert' role, as opposed to a quasi-judicial role, we have restricted our consideration to adjudications in which the adjudicator is required to comply with the rules of natural justice.

Although the situation is not entirely analogous, it is useful to consider the approach that a judge might take when one of the parties is a 'litigant in person'. Although the judge will seek to ensure that the litigant in person understands the process and the points that are being made by the opposing party (assuming that they are represented), they will be mindful of their duty of neutrality and fairness. Thus, the represented party should not be unduly prejudiced on account of the fact that the unrepresented party may not be familiar with the process.

If a party is unfamiliar with the process, it is important to ensure that the directions given as to the procedure and the applicable ground rules are clear and extensive. Things that more experienced parties would take for granted – such as not communicating with the adjudicator directly by telephone or always needing to copy in the other party when writing to the adjudicator – need to be explained. It may also be helpful to emphasize the time constraints associated with the process and the obligation to reach a Decision within the period prescribed. To this end, where there is guidance, e.g. in the form of a 'users' guide' to adjudication published by an industry body, it may be helpful to provide a copy to the parties.[1] This could be by way of an attachment to, or downloadable link within, the adjudicator's first communication with

1 For example, in the United Kingdom the Construction Industry Council publishes the *Users' Guide to Adjudication* (2017).

the parties, or perhaps at the point when it becomes apparent that one of the parties is unfamiliar with the process.

Even when clear directions are given and some form of users' guide is provided, an adjudicator might still find themselves on the end of an unsolicited telephone call or in receipt of an email that has not been copied to the opposing party. To be fair, though, this kind of mistake is not necessarily restricted to those who are unfamiliar with the process.

If an adjudicator does receive a telephone call from a party, it is important to try and end the call as soon and as politely as possible, explaining why it is necessary to do so and also asking the caller to set out any query they have in writing, copying it to the other side. Having received the call, the adjudicator should, at the earliest opportunity, record the fact a call has been received and advise the parties of the content or extent of the call, including, if possible, the approximate duration. This is in the interests of transparency and to avoid any subsequent allegations of undisclosed unilateral telephone conversations with one party.

One of the benefits of email communication is that the adjudicator can see who the email has been openly copied to. If there is no one openly copied in, this alerts the adjudicator to the possibility that it may not have been copied to the other side. In such circumstances, the adjudicator should reply and either attach or forward the email received and remind the sender, again politely, of the need to copy in all recipients. However, even when the other side is included in the list of recipients, the adjudicator may not necessarily know whether the correct email addresses have been used. For this reason, it is important for adjudicators to acknowledge communications in a timely manner as this may then reveal any incorrectly addressed emails or the fact that someone who was meant to be on the circulation list had been omitted.

In order to maintain neutrality, it is also important to refrain from providing advice to a party that goes beyond a mere explanation of the process or a point that may not be understood. However, this should not restrict the adjudicator from raising queries or putting questions to the parties, either in order to satisfy themselves that they have jurisdiction or as part of their inquisitorial powers. For example, where the contract would otherwise be excluded from the ambit of statutory adjudication, it may be that the adjudicator wishes to satisfy themselves that the parties have formally agreed to the adjudication. In these circumstances, we suggest that the adjudicator makes a simple enquiry at the outset noting that the contract appears to fall outside the scope of the applicable legislation and asking the parties either to explain the basis on which the adjudicator has jurisdiction or to confirm that they are happy for the adjudication to proceed. This should at least avoid any suggestion that it was inappropriate for the adjudicator to proceed when there was an obvious question mark over their jurisdiction. Although the represented party might be aggrieved that the adjudicator raised a point not advanced by the other party, in our view it would be wrong for an adjudicator to proceed and incur fees when they did not have a genuine belief that they had jurisdiction.

Sophisticated/represented parties

Although not all parties and representatives will have previous experience of conducting construction industry adjudications or fall into the category of being 'sophisticated' participants, for the purposes of this section we will proceed on the basis that the parties and/or representatives do have experience of the process and the applicable principles.

Even where parties do have experience and knowledge of the process, it is still important for the adjudicator to provide directions as to when and how they wish to receive submissions. In circumstances where the dispute referred is complex and/or the volume of documentation is extensive, however, it might be more appropriate to ask the parties to liaise regarding procedure and timetable and to defer to the parties' choices in this regard, ultimately being less prescriptive than an adjudicator might be with less experienced parties or representatives.

Again, although an adjudicator will have the power to raise queries or put questions to the parties, it may be safer to assume that a party represented by an experienced representative has considered the position on jurisdiction. As such, an adjudicator might not be subject to the same criticism for not raising a jurisdictional issue that had not been mentioned by the parties. Nevertheless, if there was a genuine doubt, we do not consider an adjudicator would be criticized for raising a point, especially if it would avoid incurring unnecessary cost.

In relation to queries on substantive points, again it may be perfectly acceptable for an adjudicator to restrict themselves to the arguments and materials put by the parties. However, if the adjudicator was of the view that a particular case or clause not referred to by either party was relevant to the dispute referred, it might then be appropriate to ask the parties to confirm whether or not they considered that particular case or clause was germane. The key issue in such circumstances is procedural fairness, such that the adjudicator should bring the parties' attention to something that they consider could be relevant and afford the parties the opportunity to address the point and any comments received from the opposing party.

Ex parte/uncontested proceedings

The Latin term *ex parte* is sometimes used to describe proceedings in which one of the parties does not take an active part. This will almost always be the Responding Party, but it is possible that a Referring Party may seek to discontinue proceedings and/or stop taking part on account of some intervening insolvency while the Responding Party nevertheless wishes for the adjudicator to continue. We cover insolvent parties later, but it is convenient to deal with a contested discontinuance here.

Although it is unusual, we have experienced situations in which a Referring Party has sought to discontinue an adjudication after the Referral but the Responding Party opposes this. The service of the Referral typically triggers the adjudicator's obligation to reach a Decision within a prescribed period of time. However, as will be clear by now, this is subject to an overriding obligation for a Decision to be reached in a procedurally fair manner. Additionally, there is in our view an implied duty not to incur unnecessary costs. Therefore, when deciding whether it is appropriate to proceed to reach a Decision in circumstances where the Referring Party wishes to discontinue but the Responding Party wishes the adjudicator to proceed, the adjudicator will need to consider whether it would be procedurally fair to continue and whether production of the Decision will result in unnecessary costs.

If all the substantive submissions have been made and the cost of producing the Decision will be relatively modest, then it may well be appropriate for the adjudicator to produce their Decision. Conversely, if only the Referral has been served, and assuming that the Responding Party has no issue preparing and serving a Response, the adjudicator will need to consider whether the content of the Response requires comment. If the Referring Party's position has already been articulated in the Referral and/or is set out in correspondence or documents provided with the Response, then further comment may be unnecessary. The only question then is whether the cost of reaching and publishing the Decision is merited. In this regard, it may be appropriate to canvass the parties' view as to why a Decision is or is not necessary. This will be fact dependent, but it may be that the Referring Party has conceded its claim and the Responding Party simply wishes to have the comfort or security of a temporarily binding Decision. This is all well and good, but the adjudicator may under these circumstances decide to apportion their fees such that the Responding Party pays for the provision of the Decision.

A more typical scenario is where the Responding Party does not take part but the Referring Party wishes the adjudicator to proceed. If there has been no response or interaction from the Responding Party, then the adjudicator will need to satisfy themselves that the Responding Party is aware of the proceedings. This may involve making their own enquiries and also asking the Referring Party to confirm and/or provide evidence that the Notice of Adjudication and/or the Referral was properly served. The objective will be to establish whether the failure to participate was the result of a positive election or whether it was inadvertent. We would suggest that adjudicators request read receipts for all of their emails, but where such receipts have not been provided by the Responding Party it is prudent to also request a delivery receipt. In circumstances where the Responding Party has not interacted with the adjudicator and has not provided read receipts or delivery receipts, we would suggest writing a hard-copy letter to the parties noting the lack of contact from the Responding Party and attaching copies of the relevant emails. This should be sent by a tracked delivery method where the parties are required to sign for the letter.

If the failure to participate is inadvertent, e.g. as a result of an absence or an IT issue, then that can be addressed and the proceedings brought back on track. If it is clear that the Responding Party is aware of the proceedings, it may be prudent for the adjudicator to explain that they are obliged to reach a Decision and that, if they do not hear to the contrary within a short period (24 hours, say), they shall assume that the Responding Party has made a positive decision not to take part.

In circumstances where the Responding Party has made it apparent that it does not wish to take part (or where the adjudicator has assumed this to be the position), the adjudicator should still refrain from unilateral communications and ensure that the Responding Party is still copied in on all correspondence and provided with all documents. This is in order to avoid any allegations of a failure to comply with the rules of natural justice. This applies even if the Responding Party says that it does not want to receive submissions or take part, so sensitivity might well be required. The adjudicator might wish to explain, in a respectful manner, why it is necessary to be transparent notwithstanding the Responding Party's decision not to participate.

EXAMPLE 7.1: EXAMPLE QUESTIONS PUT TO A REFERRING PARTY IN CIRCUMSTANCES WHERE THE RESPONDING PARTY IS NOT PARTICIPATING

Dear Sirs,
I ask the Referring Party to assist me with the following matters by 17:00 on Tuesday 9 January 2024.

- Please provide copies of revisions G and L of drawing number SMS 408 referred to at paragraph 1.8.37 of Appendix G of the Referral.

- I am missing the odd-numbered pages of section K10 of the specification in exhibit 23.1. Please provide a copy of these pages accordingly.

- Please provide a copy of drawing number 351-02.1 referred to in paragraph 1.23.4 of Appendix G and drawing number 352-04 referred to in paragraph 1.23.6.

- Please provide a copy of EAI 147, which is not contained in Appendix H of the Referral.

- My understanding from the breakdown of Western's invoices is that, to date, it has only invoiced for work undertaken in respect of the following EAIs:

  - EAI 23 in invoices 1729 and 1733;
  - EAI's 39, 42 and 46 in invoice 1856;
  - EAI's 32.1, 32.5, 35.1, 35.6 and 49 in invoice 1882.

If my understanding is correct, on what basis does the Referring Party say that it is entitled for work undertaken by Western against other EAIs?

- Of the 34 DCL items that the Referring Party contends relate to Changes, only nine refer to EAIs: namely, the items against invoices 56, 57, 58A, 58B, 61 and 62. Please clarify which EAIs the other items relate to.

Yours faithfully,

...

Even though one party may not participate, this does not excuse the adjudicator from assessing the submissions and evidence in order to determine whether the redress sought should be granted. The party seeking relief will therefore still have the burden of making out its case and persuading the adjudicator that it is entitled to the relief sought. This may involve the adjudicator seeking clarification or provision of further documentation, or even inviting comment on matters that the adjudicator considers relevant. Although in uncontested proceedings the evidential burden may be set at a relatively low level, this does not necessarily mean that the unopposed party will be successful in obtaining the relief sought.

Insolvent parties

When we refer to insolvent parties, we mean a situation in which a party is subject to formal insolvency arrangements, as distinct from a party who claims to be insolvent. There are two main situations where the insolvency of parties may be encountered. The first is when one of the parties is already insolvent at the outset. The second is where one of the parties becomes insolvent during the course of proceedings. In either of these two situations, the appropriate course of action can differ depending on whether the insolvent party is the Referring Party or the Responding Party.

If it is the Referring Party that is insolvent, the adjudicator will need to satisfy themselves that the relevant insolvency practitioner has authorized the proceedings to commence and/or be continued and has also made sufficient provision for payment of the adjudicator's fees and expenses in the event that the claim is unsuccessful. The authority point is obvious, and making provision for payment of fees is necessary to avoid any unfairness: although the parties will be jointly and severally liable for the adjudicator's fees, it cannot be fair for an insolvent party to pursue adjudication proceedings knowing that it will never be liable for the adjudicator's fees.

If it is the Responding Party that is insolvent, the adjudicator will need to obtain confirmation from the insolvency practitioner that they are content for the proceedings to continue – and, if so, the adjudicator will need to find out whether they wish to participate. This is because, typically, insolvent parties can be afforded statutory protection from claims being pursued. In the event such protection is in place and is not waived by the insolvency practitioner, the adjudicator will be obliged to stand down. If this is the case, the adjudicator might look to the solvent party to pay for any fees incurred for time spent on the matter. Whether a fee is charged is ultimately a commercial decision for the adjudicator. Perhaps no fee will be charged if the time spent has been minimal, whereas if the adjudicator's involvement is more extensive, on account of having to address administrative or procedural matters and/or substantive submissions, an adjudicator might consider themselves justified in charging for their time.

Where the Responding Party's insolvency practitioner has confirmed that they are content for the adjudication to continue, they will also need to confirm whether they wish to participate. If they do, then, as for the situation with an insolvent Referring Party, they will need to confirm that they have made provision for payment of the adjudicator's fees. In our experience, however, it is more common for insolvent Responding Parties not to take an active part following the appointment of an insolvency practitioner, but to instead confirm that they are happy for proceedings to continue. In such circumstances, the adjudicator should seek confirmation from the Referring Party that they are still happy for the adjudication to proceed in the knowledge that they are likely to have to pay for the adjudicator's fees in the first instance irrespective of the outcome. Although the Responding Party may be insolvent, there may be good reason for continuing with an adjudication, e.g. if the Referring Party has the benefit of a guarantee or bond that pays out on an adjudicator's Decision in a beneficiary's favour.

Even if the Responding Party elects not to participate, then, as for other types of uncontested proceedings, the adjudicator should ensure that all communications, and ultimately their Decision, are copied to the Responding Party's representative and/or the appointed insolvency practitioner.

TYPES OF DISPUTE

Large/complex disputes

We already touched on initial procedural considerations when we discussed the timetable for large or complex disputes in chapter 3. Within this section we share our experiences of the types of dispute that may fall into this category.

When we use the term 'large', we are alluding to the volume of issues and documents that might have to be considered. An example of a large dispute would be a final account dispute in which there are a significant number of unagreed variations or changes where liability and/or quantum are in issue, where there are differences between the parties concerning liability for delays, and where there are allegations of defective design and workmanship. This type of adjudication is colloquially referred to as a 'kitchen-sink adjudication'.

The starting point for these type of dispute is to establish and reconcile the parties' respective positions such that there is a clear agenda for the adjudicator's Decision. While the parties might already have set out their respective positions for the adjudicator, this is not always the case, and it can sometimes feel as if the parties' positions are like ships passing in the night! In such circumstances, the adjudicator may task the parties with providing a reconciliation of the key issues or, alternatively, seek clarification either via correspondence or at a meeting. This may also be the case if the parties' positions change during the course of an adjudication as a result of concessions or agreements reached on discrete items.

We address the various elements that might form part of a kitchen-sink adjudication separately under distinct headings of extension of time, variations, loss and/or expense/damages, and defects later in this chapter. However, where a Referring Party has elected to package up all of the elements, the adjudicator will need to decide which order to address those elements in. This will be case or fact dependent, and it might be that the elements can be addressed independently of one another. The priority or order in which the adjudicator addresses issues may then be a matter of personal preference or it could be based on the fact that submissions on a particular element are more advanced. For example, if a claim for prolongation costs is premised on compensable delays being caused by variations the liability for which is disputed, the adjudicator is likely to need to address the variation account first.

The ability to identify the issues that are to be determined and the order in which they fall to be addressed is a key function of the adjudicator. In view of the importance of this function, we address in more detail how this can be done in chapter 8.

Low-value disputes

The perception of what constitutes a 'low-value dispute' may vary. A $100,000 dispute might be considered low value by a large organization but high value by a private individual or a small company. For present purposes the upper limit is not particularly important save to say that dealing with low-value disputes provides a particular challenge for the adjudicator because of the potential for the level of the adjudicator's fees to be disproportionate to the sum in dispute.

Although certain administrative tasks may not vary between high-value and low-value disputes, in that certain costs may be relatively fixed, the amount of time required by an adjudicator will depend on a variety of factors including the volume of documentation provided, the number of submissions, the complexity of the subject matter and the conduct of the parties. Just because a dispute is low in value does not mean that the subject matter is of low complexity or that there will be a low volume of documentation provided. Although the adjudicator may have some control over the number or size of submissions, this might be more difficult to control at the outset of the proceedings, and, if a Referring Party elects to make detailed submissions and provide extensive documentation in a Referral, it may be necessary for the responsive submissions and supporting documents to be similarly extensive in order to address the dispute that has been referred.

As a result of concerns regarding the level of adjudicators' fees that might be incurred for low-value disputes, a number of schemes have been put in place in the United Kingdom that effectively either act as a fee-capping scheme or restrict the volume of documents and the number of submissions. Examples of this are the TECSA Low Value Disputes adjudication service and the Construction Industry Council Low Value Dispute Module Adjudication Procedure. Both of these schemes cap the overall amount an adjudicator can charge based on the value of the dispute, and the latter scheme also restricts the number and volume of submissions.

Variations/changes

Disputes concerning variations or changes can vary from a dispute over a single item or a greater number of items falling within a disputed interim or final account. They can also relate to liability, purely quantum or both.

Where multiple variation claims have been referred to adjudication, the adjudicator will need to consider the extent to which it is possible and/or necessary to address all of the variations referred within the timetable which has either been set or agreed. The time required may differ depending on whether the dispute referred concerns an interim or final account and whether there will be an opportunity for the parties to re-address the valuation of a disputed variation in a later payment cycle. It may therefore be that a Decision only represents a determination of the value in respect of a specific interim payment cycle and not for all further payment cycles.

Although it will vary, we find that where there are a large number of variations in dispute, e.g. hundreds or even thousands, it may be that the adjudicator elects to address them in a schedule which is attached to the main body of their Decision. If there are recurring issues, it may be that these lend themselves to a fuller explanation within the main body of the Decision, with briefer comments set out in the accompanying schedule[2]. Alternatively, the adjudicator may wish to deal with the higher value or more complex variations in the main body of their Decision with the remainder in the schedule. However, if the number of variations are manageable and do not make the Decision unwieldy, it may be that each variation is addressed within the main body of the Decision. Ultimately, this will be a matter of the adjudicator's personal preference.

---

2 Refer to appendix C for an example schedule dealing with variations

We sometimes find that a sampling approach is adopted, either at the suggestion of the adjudicator or the parties. This may be particularly appropriate if the difference purely relates to quantum or valuation. If a sampling approach is to be adopted it is important that the adjudicator makes it clear how the process will work. This may involve consultation with the parties and agreement as to which variations in dispute will fall to be assessed and how any findings are to be extrapolated or applied to the non-selected variations. For example, each party may select a certain number and/or the adjudicator is left to select a random sample. Alternatively, the selection might simply be based on the difference between the parties' valuations of the variations.

EXAMPLE 7.2: EXAMPLE OF SAMPLING PROCEDURE AGREED BY THE PARTIES

An example of a sampling procedure agreed by parties to an adjudication is as follows:

> The parties agree that all variations where the difference between their valuations exceeds £1,000.00 will be individually assessed by an adjudicator and that, once the adjudicator has completed their valuation of these variations and calculated the total value ('the Total Assessed Value'), they should then
>
> - calculate the percentage that the Total Assessed Value bears to the total value claimed by the Referring Party for these variations ('the Total Claimed Value'); and
> - apply the resulting percentage ('the Assessed Percentage') to the Referring Party's valuation of the variations that have not been individually assessed by the adjudicator.

We also sometimes find that the parties are amenable to removing some of the variations in dispute by agreeing a compromise where the difference is low. This can sometimes be effected by a prompt from the adjudicator indicating how much time it will take to address each one of the variations in dispute. However, again, in our view it is important that the parties' agreement is obtained.

Extensions of time

Disputes over the culpability for delays encountered on construction projects are commonplace. We find that they can give rise to legal, factual and technical issues. Typically, legal issues can concern questions of whether a particular delay event falls within the ambit of an extension of time clause or whether provision of notice constitutes a condition precedent. Factual issues can involve questions of whether valid notice of delay has been given and, most significantly, whether or not a particular event caused completion of the project to be delayed and/or gives rise to an entitlement to an extension of time. Technical issues primarily involve consideration of whether an assessment of delay or methodology is appropriate, but they can also involve a host of other technical considerations that may be related to the factual issues. Ultimately, disputes regarding delays can be some of the most complex an adjudicator has to deal with.

It should be remembered that what might need to be provided under the underlying contract to support a claim for an extension of time is likely to differ from what might need to be provided to an adjudicator. Typically, what is required under a contract is some form of notification, an assessment of the extent or likely delay, and any supporting particulars. This will then likely trigger an assessment by someone who is tasked with that role and who will have knowledge of the project, e.g. the architect, engineer or project manager. In contrast, the adjudicator's involvement will normally only start once the dispute as to time has arisen, and they will then be required to act in a quasi-judicial manner. The party advancing the claim will therefore need to persuade the adjudicator that they are entitled to an extension of time, and this will often require them to provide submissions and evidence in support of their claim that go beyond the particularization requirements of the contract.

Although not all extension of time claims rely on supporting delay analysis, all but the simplest cases do, in our experience. If a party has the technical expertise to conduct a delay analysis in-house, then they may choose not to rely on an external expert to support their case. However, even if a contractor has programming resource in-house, programmers are typically focused on planning how a project can be delivered rather than conducting or presenting a delay analysis in support of a claim for an extension of time. For this reason, we often see delay analysts employed as experts by parties when advancing or defending extension of time claims.

When parties engage expert delay analysts (or, for that matter, any expert) in adjudication, unlike in other forums, such as arbitration or litigation, there is little opportunity for the experts to meet to discuss methodology, the appropriate baseline programme, their competing views, etc. Similarly, the experts engaged by each party may be limited in their access to documents and also the time available to undertake assessments. This can result in the instructions given to the opposing experts differing; in particular, the instructions given to an expert engaged by a Responding Party might be limited to a critique of the report or analysis prepared by the expert employed by the Referring Party.

Where the experts agree that a particular methodology of delay analysis is appropriate, any issues may be focused on whether the analysis has been undertaken correctly or whether the facts relied upon are correct. Conversely, where the methodology adopted differs or is not agreed as being correct, the adjudicator will need to decide which methodology to adopt – and ultimately, parties and their experts often refer adjudicators to the Society of Construction Law's Delay and Disruption Protocol to justify their preferred methodology.[3] The methodology adopted is important as it will affect the analysis and also potentially the routemap for the part of the adjudicator's Decision that deals with delays. When faced with competing positions, it may be that the adjudicator asks the parties' experts to explain to the adjudicator why their methodology is appropriate. This can be done in writing or in person, and we will sometimes call meetings specifically to address delay-related issues that will include, as an agenda item, the appropriate method of delay analysis to be adopted. However, it is important to note that if the adjudicator prefers the methodology adopted by one expert, it does not automatically follow that the opinion of the other expert is of no value: the other expert's views on the causes of delay, etc., may still be of assistance in determining the extension of time due.

3 Society of Construction Law. 2017. *Delay and Disruption Protocol*, 2nd edition (February).

Once a method of delay analysis is decided upon, it will be a matter of working through the parties' respective positions in order to determine what caused or is likely to have caused the delay and/or whether it gives rise to an entitlement. This may involve reference to factual evidence in order to determine the state of progress at particular dates. Once the cause (or causes) of delay is (or are) established, it is a matter of the adjudicator applying their findings on any liability issues to the delay analysis and then proceeding to a conclusion on any entitlement to an extension of time.

Loss and/or expense/damages

In general terms, disputes concerning claims for loss and/or expense or damages either concern those associated with time-related matters or disruption. Although an entitlement to additional time does not necessarily result in a corresponding entitlement to additional money, it often does, and when it does, it follows that it may be necessary to consider the underlying entitlement to additional time before it is possible to address causation and/or quantum of a monetary claim. The same principle may apply to a claim for liquidated or delay damages where the claim is defended on the basis of an alleged entitlement to an extension of time.

Sometimes a party defending a claim for prolongation loss and/or expense will seek to assert that there were concurrent or parallel delays that the contractor was responsible for such that they are not entitled to prolongation costs during the periods of concurrency. They will argue that the claiming party cannot demonstrate that, but for the delay events that gave rise to an entitlement to an extension of time, they would not have incurred prolongation costs for the same periods; this is because such costs would have been incurred in any event due to the contractor's own culpable delay. This may therefore require further consideration of a delay analysis in order to reach a conclusion on the applicable periods for assessment for prolongation costs, as well as dealing with the law on concurrency, which, at least when it comes to the United Kingdom, is by no means settled. Once the applicable period for the assessment of prolongation costs is determined, it will be a case of assessing the parties' positions on quantum and the supporting evidence.

Claims for disruption are typically premised on the basis that, because of a qualifying event and/or breach on the part of the other party, disruption was encountered and resulted in additional costs or losses being incurred. The starting point will be to establish whether there has actually been disruption. If disruption is established, it will then be a matter of assessing whether losses or additional costs have been incurred as a result. This can be a difficult task for a claiming party, and it will typically involve an assessment of what time or cost should have been required to undertake an activity, together with an assessment of the additional time or cost the claiming party contends was actually incurred. This will ultimately be a question of the evidence being evaluated by the adjudicator.

Disruption claims, and to a lesser extent prolongation claims, can sometimes be packaged or advanced as global claims, and in our experience there are often arguments over both the current law applying to global claims in different jurisdictions and whether the claim in question constitutes a global claim at all.

Defects

Disputes concerning defects can either be in the context of deductions applied against a claim for payment for work done or as a standalone claim arising either during the construction phase of a project or post completion. These types of claim will involve the party that is alleging defects needing to establish that there has been a breach in terms of a non-conformance with a requirement of the contract and that, as a consequence, it has incurred (or will incur) a loss. These claims will typically involve technical evidence, sometimes, but not always, provided by independent experts, and they will require the adjudicator to reach a finding as to whether there has been a breach or a defect exists. If a defect is established, the adjudicator may then be required to address the question of what is the appropriate means of rectifying the defect, the costs of the rectification works, and whether a party is entitled to recover and/or make a deduction for such costs.

Contra charges/other deductions

As well as deductions on account of defects it is not uncommon to encounter 'contra charges' or deductions for other matters that a paying party may seek to apply to the valuation of an account. Again, the party seeking to make a deduction will have the burden of making out its case in respect of having a legal entitlement to make a deduction and also the amount of that deduction. Typical deductions we see are claims for supplementing labour or procurement of items on behalf of the other party.

Legal/contractual interpretation

Disputes concerning the interpretation of a contract can arise in the context of many of the other categories of dispute discussed in this chapter. However, contractual interpretation can sometimes also – when it is permissible – constitute the entire extent of the matter that has been referred. The principles of interpretation of a contract will very much be jurisdiction specific, and the adjudicator will have to consider the parties' competing legal submissions in support of the interpretations contended. In our experience, this can sometimes result in an interpretation that is not precisely aligned with either party's interpretation. The extent to which an adjudicator is entitled to make an alternative declaration to that sought may be dependent on the applicable legislation or procedural rules as well as the scope of the declarations sought. However, this should not preclude an adjudicator making an alternative finding, and it may be that the ultimate decision is that a declaration sought is not granted.

Payment notice disputes

These types of dispute concern claims for payment that is alleged to be due as a result of the non-payment of a notified sum. The notified sum may be provided by the payer or, in some instances, by the party seeking payment ('the payee'). In the United Kingdom, adjudications that address these latter types of claim are colloquially known as 'smash and grab' adjudications. As payment notice disputes will be dependent on the correct type and timing of written notices, they lend themselves to a documents-only procedure. However, even then we have encountered expert IT consultant evidence (including making provision for inspection of computer equipment/hard drives) where there is a question mark over whether or not an electronic communication or notice was sent or received, and if so, when.

Professional negligence

To the extent a contract with a construction professional also constitutes a contract that provides for adjudication, either because it represents a qualifying construction contract pursuant to the applicable legislation or as a matter of an express contract provision, this may give rise to claims that the professional has failed to exercise the standard of reasonable skill and care required of them. Therefore, although these types of claim are labelled as 'professional negligence' claims, they are typically advanced as contractual claims.

A common feature of claims against professionals is that expert evidence is likely to be advanced and/or required in all bar the most obvious of cases. Another common feature is that professionals are likely to have some form of professional indemnity insurance that can add an additional layer of complexity into the process, even if the insurer's involvement is not disclosed. Our experience is that the parties are also likely to involve specialist/experienced solicitors and potentially also counsel.

Where the parties have engaged experts who have provided conflicting opinions on whether a professional has fallen below the required standard of reasonable skill and care, in our experience it will sometimes be helpful to hear from the experts and to ask questions. Where counsel is engaged by both parties, it may be that the adjudicator allows counsel a set period of time for questioning. However, even if such an approach is adopted, we consider that an adjudicator should afford themselves the opportunity to put questions on points that would assist them.

As well as a determination of liability the adjudicator may also be required to reach a decision on quantum. This may be within the same adjudication dealing with liability, or, sometimes, it might follow a previous adjudicator's Decision in which liability has already been determined. If liability and quantum are included in the same adjudication, it may still be necessary to address quantum issues in a meeting with the parties so that any queries can be clarified and also to assess how much time the adjudicator might need to determine quantum in the event liability is established. However, where liability has already been determined, the adjudicator's task will be limited to addressing any issues between the parties, such as the extent to which the losses claimed are recoverable, causation and/or evidence of loss.

Hybrid contracts

The term 'hybrid' is used to describe contracts that involve some operations that give rise to a statutory right to refer disputes to adjudication and some that do not. Examples of these types of contract exist under the UK legislation that provides exceptions for certain activities (but not all activities) where the primary activity is power generation, e.g. the installation of plant or machinery. This has given rise to an additional layer of complexity for both parties and the adjudicator where a jurisdictional challenge is raised, and this may mean that an adjudicator is only entitled to address disputes that relate to the 'non-excluded' operations.

If a party refers only the 'non-excluded' operations, there should not be any issue. However, if the question of whether the matters referred constitute 'non-excluded' operations is contentious, then we would recommend that the adjudicator addresses this as a preliminary jurisdictional issue. Likewise, if there is a mix of excluded and 'non-excluded' operations, the adjudicator should determine the extent of the matters that they can consider as a preliminary jurisdictional issue and advise the parties of their conclusion. Having done this, the subsequent submissions can be focused on any matters that the adjudicator confirms they consider to be within their jurisdiction.

Joinder/consolidation of multiparty proceedings

Although unusual, we have seen some contracts that provide for consolidation or joinder of disputes arising from separate but related contracts between different parties. For example, a main contractor may wish to join or involve a subcontractor or consultant in an adjudication where they are facing a claim that relates to work undertaken by that subcontractor or consultant. The key is for all parties to all of the separate contracts to agree to such arrangements. This can either be as a result of express provisions in the separate contracts or by way of ad hoc agreements entered into by the parties after the dispute (or disputes) has (or have) arisen.

Even if the parties do not agree a consolidation of the adjudications, they may agree for them to run in parallel. In the event of an ad hoc agreement, we would advise that the adjudicator sets out a procedure and invites the parties to agree to it. Some essential elements of the procedure include the following.

- Clarification of whether the adjudications have been consolidated or are to remain separate adjudications running in parallel.

- If the parties agree that the adjudications are to remain separate but run in parallel, where there is a restriction on adjudicators acting at the same time on related disputes under different contracts – such as there is in the United Kingdom under paragraph 8(1) of the Scheme – the agreement will need to include confirmation that each party gives their consent to the adjudicator acting in the parallel adjudications.

- An agreement that each party waives confidentiality between themselves in respect of each of the adjudications (assuming they remain separate adjudications).

- The procedure and timetable for the submissions, with careful consideration of the order of those submissions. For example, if a main contractor is responding to a defects claim from an employer, the main contractor may need to receive submissions in a parallel adjudication against a subcontractor before responding to the employer.

CHAPTER 8

Identifying issues

As already mentioned in the previous chapter, the ability to identify the issues that are to be determined and the order in which they fall to be addressed is an essential skill that is needed by all adjudicators.

WHAT IS AN ISSUE?

We like to think of an issue as being something that needs to be decided in order to determine the dispute referred and to decide whether or not to grant the redress sought. There are two aspects to this. First, there must be a difference between the parties on the point. Second, it must be necessary to decide the point in order to reach the Decision. To be clear on this second point, not all matters that are in dispute between the parties may fall to be decided. This may be because they are not relevant, because they are not determinative of the dispute referred, and/or because they are contingent on a particular finding in respect of a preceding issue.

An example of an irrelevant matter could be a disagreement as to whether it was raining or not on a particular day when a timesheet was signed. Although the extent to which a recollection was correct may be relevant when assessing a witness's ability to recall a specific event, it may not be relevant when assessing whether the timesheet was signed at all. An example of a contingent issue could be in the context of a claim for a variation where the adjudicator decides that an item does not constitute a variation at all, such that it is not necessary to proceed to determine any valuation or quantum issues.

TIPS FOR FORMULATING ISSUES

Two main factors need to be considered when formulating issues: the redress sought and the parties' positions. Although it may be possible to predict what the issues may be from a description of the dispute in the Notice of Adjudication or the Referral, until the parties' positions are known it is not possible for the issues to be fully formulated.

In an ideal world, the Notice of Adjudication, or even the Referral, would include a full description of the dispute and both of the parties' positions, but in our experience this is rare. This is especially so in the United Kingdom, where the courts have made it clear that the Referring Party is entitled to advance new arguments and evidence and the Responding Party is entitled to advance any legitimate available defences provided that, in both instances, the other party has a reasonable opportunity to consider the new arguments, etc. Consequently, and more typically, it is not until after the Response that a first draft of the issues to be addressed can be formulated. Thereafter, these issues may fall to be developed or refined as further submissions are made, or even while the adjudicator is drafting their Decision.

In the context of an issue representing a matter that falls to be decided, we think that an issue should be posed as a question that requires an answer. Having reviewed the written submission(s), then, a good starting point for formulating the issues that fall to be addressed, at least at a high level, is the redress sought. So, if the redress sought is posed as a declaration that 'the valuation of application for payment 1 is $100,000 or such other sum that the adjudicator decides', then, assuming that the value is not accepted, this could be formulated as the following question: 'What is the correct value of application for payment 1?' However, note that this will inevitably be only the starting point: it is likely that the differences in valuation will be made up of a number of items or 'sub-issues'. This will obviously require a more in-depth analysis of the parties' positions in order to identify what the differences are and, thereafter, the reason(s) for those differences. This will in turn enable a full list of issues to be formulated.

How the parties' differences are identified will be a matter of personal choice. One approach we are aware of is to highlight relevant sentences of the submissions in different colours based on whether the submission is agreed or denied. The elements that have been highlighted as denied can then be assessed as to whether they are relevant to the redress sought, such that they represent a matter to be determined.

Where the responsive submissions address the previous submissions on a paragraph-by-paragraph basis, whether in whole or in part, we are aware that some adjudicators will prepare a working document, as either a spreadsheet or a schedule/table, in almost a 'Scott schedule' type format.[1] The parties' competing arguments are put into the document so they can be included in a consolidated submission that can be analysed, perhaps even with a column added in which the adjudicator can make notes.

Where the submissions do not mirror each other or do not respond on a paragraph-by-paragraph basis, this may not lend itself to highlighting or production of a consolidated submissions document. In such instances, it may just be a case of good old-fashioned note taking!

Once the differences have been identified and the issues and sub-issues have been formulated, the next step will be to decide in which order the issues fall to be addressed. This may be a matter of following an obvious logical sequence, where the determination of an issue is required before a subsequent issue would need to be addressed, as in the following example.

(i) **Issue 1**. Has there been a breach of contract?

(ii) **Issue 2**. If so, has the breach caused recoverable loss?

(iii) **Issue 3.** If so, how much loss?

Alternatively, if the issues are independent of each other, they could be addressed in an order either that suits the adjudicator or that takes into account the fact that the parties' submissions on certain issues may have concluded while other aspects remain ongoing. Ultimately, the adjudicator will have discretion over the order in which the issues are addressed.

1 A "Scott Schedule" is a schedule setting the parties' respective positions on each disputed item in a table format. It takes its name from George Scott KC, a UK Official Referee from 1920 to 1933.

EXAMPLE 8.1: EXAMPLE LIST OF ISSUES IN A FINAL ACCOUNT DISPUTE

Issue 1. On what date was Practical Completion of the Works achieved?

Issue 2. To what date should the Period for Completion be adjusted?

- *Sub-issue A*. Did the Project Manager agree an extension of time to 29 October 2023 in respect of the Revision 5 Programme?
- *Sub-issue B*. What is the appropriate methodology for determining the critical path and analysing the delays?
- *Sub-issue C*. Where did the critical path run between 5 July 2021 and the date on which Practical Completion was achieved?
- *Sub-issue D*. What is the extent of the Referring Party's extension of time entitlement?

Issue 3. What is the true value of the final account?

- *Sub-issue A*. What is the true value of the measured works?
- *Sub-issue B*. What is the true value of the Instructed Variations?
- *Sub-issue C*. What is the true value of the Uninstructed Variations?
- *Sub-issue D*. What is the true value of the Prolongation?
- *Sub-issue E*. What is the true value of the Disruption?

Issue 4. Is the Referring Party entitled to payment in this adjudication and, if so, how much and when is it due?

CANVASSING THE PARTIES' VIEWS

Some adjudicators may seek to canvass the parties' views on the issues. This may not be appropriate where the parties are not sufficiently experienced, but it might still be appropriate for the adjudicator to share their own formulation or understanding of the issues with the parties so that they have the opportunity to comment. In the past we have invited the parties to liaise regarding the issues, although this tended to be in the earlier days of our practice: it is not something we do much now as we are more experienced in formulating issues and selecting the order in which they fall to be addressed. That said, if there was a lack of clarity or some uncertainty regarding the scope of our jurisdiction, we would not rule this out. The advantage of sharing our understanding or inviting the parties' views is that it may reduce the scope for complaint or inadvertent error. The disadvantage is that it may involve the parties in additional cost and could lead to a 'satellite' dispute between the parties regarding what the issues are or should be.

If a meeting is being held, then adding a short agenda item for the adjudicator to share their understanding of the issues with the parties may be a sensible way of addressing any uncertainty. This is especially so if one of the reasons the adjudicator called the meeting was because of a lack of clarity regarding the parties' positions and the matters to be determined.

LIST OF OBSERVATIONS AND ISSUES

We are aware of one very experienced adjudicator who sets out a detailed list of observations and issues. As we understand it, at a relatively early stage – either post Referral or post Response – the adjudicator will provide a commentary on the matters referred and the submissions and will invite the parties to comment or to respond to specific questions. This represents an example of an adjudicator 'rolling up their sleeves' – it is very much a hands-on approach to the investigation of a dispute. Adjudicators invariably have inquisitorial powers and adopting such an approach would ordinarily fall within the scope of such powers.

Whether the adoption of an approach in which the adjudicator publishes a list of observations and issues is appropriate and/or will result in a more cost-efficient process will probably depend on the nature of the dispute and also the parties' expectations. If the parties are aware that the adjudicator is likely to adopt a particular approach, they can then tailor their submissions to suit that approach. We can certainly see advantages for the parties in having an indication of the adjudicator's thoughts so that they can address them in advance of the Decision being made, but we can also see how responding to the adjudicator's observations and issues might also increase the costs to the parties and result in more submissions than would otherwise have been made.

Although it is not an entirely analogous situation, we are aware of at least one instance in the United Kingdom where an adjudicator shared a 'provisional' Decision with the parties and invited comments. This unfortunately subsequently led to arguments in the High Court (and then in the Court of Appeal) based on a claim that the adjudicator had predetermined the dispute or had closed their mind to the parties' submissions. We would not, therefore, recommend adopting such an approach, even though, ultimately, the adjudicator's Decision was enforced.

RELEVANT CASE LAW

In the UK case of *Lanes Group Plc v Galliford Try Infrastructure Ltd*,[2] the adjudicator issued a 'Preliminary Views Document' before he had received the Responding Party's (i.e. Lanes's) Response. In the High Court, Lanes argued that there was apparent bias because the adjudicator had, in effect, already made up his mind before he had seen the Response.

The judge held that the Preliminary Views Document read like a draft Decision. He said that it gave the impression that the adjudicator had already made up his mind and that the words of qualification in it did not remove the overriding impression that a Decision had already been made. Accordingly, the judge was satisfied that there had been apparent bias towards Galliford Try and declined to enforce the Decision.

On appeal, however, the Court of Appeal found that there was no apparent bias, since a fair-minded observer would characterize the Preliminary Views Document as a provisional view for the assistance of the parties and not as a final determination. Galliford Try's appeal was therefore successful.

MARSHALLING SUBMISSIONS AND EVIDENCE

Once the adjudicator has formulated the list of issues and sub-issues, the next step will be the production of the Decision, which we discuss in the next chapter. However, before starting the drafting of the Decision we recommend adjudicators take the time to marshal the submissions and evidence so that they can identify in which paragraphs of

2 [2011] EWHC 1679 (TCC).

the submissions, including the expert reports and witness statements, the parties' cases on the issues and sub-issues can be found. Trying to remember where the parties' cases on a particular point are set out when there are hundreds, or even thousands, of pages of submissions can be a near-impossible task. There is therefore a very real risk that something will be missed. We certainly find that creating a type of route map to the submissions makes navigating around the documents a lot less daunting, and while it results in longer preparation time prior to getting down to actually writing the Decision, time savings are made overall.

Some adjudicators create the route map to the submissions by making notes, but we would advocate a more structured approach whereby the submission references are entered into a schedule. We provide an example of such a schedule in appendix D, and we would stress that this is generally a 'live' document that can be altered during the course of writing the Decision.

CHAPTER 9

The Decision

The fact that it has taken until chapter 9 of this book to get to the Decision is testimony to the fact that the function of the adjudicator is not solely about the production of a Decision. That said, the production of a Decision is arguably the most important part of the job. It represents the end product of the adjudicator's work and the output of the adjudication of the dispute that was referred.

Before addressing the content and structure of a Decision and how an adjudicator may go about deciding the dispute that has been referred, it is useful to highlight the fact that one of the reasons an adjudicator's Decision might not eventually be enforced by a court is a material breach of natural justice on the part of the adjudicator. This is why it is so important for the adjudicator to be mindful of what historic or current involvements may represent a conflict of interest (such that it would be inappropriate to act, or to continue to act) and also to be aware of, and sufficiently versed in, their duty to conduct the adjudication in a procedurally fair manner. It is also for this reason that we have afforded so much of this book to these aspects.

Although there is a view that the adjudicator is under an obligation to produce an *enforceable* Decision – and while we recognize that the extent to which a Decision is enforceable may be dependent on the adjudicator's conduct – the question of enforceability may actually be totally independent of anything the adjudicator was either made aware of or could control. That said, we believe that an adjudicator should aspire to conduct themselves in such a manner that they do not undermine the enforceability of a Decision. However, even if they do, a court might take a different view, and this reflects the complexity of the process, the time-limited nature of adjudication, and the associated pressures imposed on the adjudicator and the parties. Therefore, the fact that a judge might, with the benefit of both hindsight and skilful submissions, reach a different conclusion on a jurisdictional issue is perhaps understandable.

Just because a Decision is unenforceable does not mean that it represents a poor piece of work. Conversely, the fact that a Decision is enforceable does not necessarily mean that it represents a good piece of work. Although the way different adjudicators present or prepare their Decisions will vary on account of individual styles or preferences, we nevertheless consider that there are some fundamental basic principles that should be followed by adjudicators and that can be considered to represent good practice.

WHO IS THE ADJUDICATOR WRITING THE DECISION FOR?

The obvious answer to this question is 'the parties'. However, if we think about the different types of party that may be involved with a construction contract, there could be a wide range of sizes and types of organazations, as well as individuals, who fall under the umbrella term 'parties'. Indeed, the 'party' umbrella may also extend to include advisors, representatives or professionals employed by a party, in connection with either the adjudication or the construction contract or project itself.

Similarly, if we think about the types of organization that could be a party to an adjudication, the individuals involved in the day-to-day running of the adjudication may well not be those who own or who have ultimate management responsibility for that organization. The short point to make is that, just because an organization is a party to an adjudication, it does not mean that all individuals employed or engaged by that organization will have knowledge of either the subject matter or the conduct of the adjudication. However, those individuals may have cause to read the Decision in order to implement its effect or to seek advice in that respect.

Whether or not a party to an adjudication is familiar with the process and/or the underlying subject matter is also often relevant. For instance, in terms of writing style, what is appropriate for a large corporate organization represented by experienced lawyers is likely to be different to what is appropriate for a small 'jobbing' builder or consumer who is not familiar with construction industry disputes and who has represented themselves.

It is sometimes said that the party that has been successful in an adjudication will be less interested in the Decision than the losing party, given their success. We are not sure this is entirely correct because a successful party will still need to consider the extent to which the Decision is enforceable and/or whether the Decision is likely to represent the final outcome in the event the unsuccessful party elects to refer the dispute to arbitration or litigation. However, it is probably fair to say that the unsuccessful party will have greater motivation to consider the Decision and subject it to greater scrutiny. For this reason, the focus of many adjudicators when they are writing their Decision is the losing party. One theory is that if a party knows and can understand why they have lost and can see that all of their arguments have been considered, they are more likely to 'live with' the Decision, even on a temporary basis and even if they do not agree with the adjudicator's findings.

Although adjudicators may seek to take account of the parties' advisors or representatives when drafting the Decision, it should be noted that those advisors or representatives are not always disclosed. For example, we are aware that some parties will engage experts or legal counsel to advise on discrete issues without sharing that fact with the adjudicator or the other party. Additionally, the parties may seek advice after the Decision is published, e.g. on the enforceability or the correctness of the Decision. This may also involve consideration of how the adjudication was conducted. So we yet again come to a situation in which the reader of the Decision may not necessarily have a familiarity with the subject matter or have been involved with the adjudication itself.

Another reader who could be considered to be new to the dispute and the adjudication is the judge who is required to determine whether the Decision is enforceable. In our experience, it is unusual for an adjudicator to be asked to attend – or provide evidence in – enforcement proceedings. The Decision may therefore be the only opportunity an adjudicator has to explain to a judge how and why they have conducted the adjudication in a particular way or to provide an explanation of the scope of the matters considered.

The Decision may also be read by individuals within professional bodies or ANAs/ANBs who are required to address any complaints advanced against an adjudicator or to assess an adjudicator's competence, either as part of a periodic reassessment process or as part of the assessment process to recruit or appoint adjudicators to their panels or rosters. In the case of both reassessment and assessment, we are aware that some organizations will ask for a number of previous Decisions to be provided on a confidential basis. This will usually require Decisions to be redacted or the names of individuals or details of the project to be changed in order to preserve confidentiality.

If we think about the range of individuals who might have cause to read a Decision and the fact that not all readers will have been involved with the adjudication itself, it is clear why a Decision needs to provide a more detailed explanation than perhaps might have been required if the Decision was only being written for those with knowledge of the subject matter and the adjudication process itself.

NATURAL JUSTICE CONSIDERATIONS

As we have already mentioned, the Decision is likely to be the only opportunity an adjudicator has for providing an explanation of what happened or why they elected to conduct an adjudication in a particular way. The adjudicator should set out any objections raised to their impartiality or the procedure adopted, and they should include an explanation of the actions taken. They must also be aware that their Decision may be subject to scrutiny in relation to their actions in deciding the substantive issues. In particular, the court may be interested in whether the adjudicator reached their Decision based on an argument or methodology not advanced by the parties, whether the adjudicator had failed to take into account all of the defences advanced, and so on. When these issues are taken into consideration, it is clear why it is important for a Decision to cover both the procedural and the substantive aspects of the adjudication in sufficient detail to enable an uninvolved reader to understand the approach adopted and the Decision made.

STRUCTURE

The structure of a Decision will again be a matter of personal choice, but we generally tend to see two types of approach: one that is more legal in nature, having the appearance of an arbitration award or a judgment; and a second that is more akin to a professional or expert report. To the best of our knowledge, there are no mandatory requirements for the form of a Decision (other than, perhaps, that it is rendered in writing). While there may be mandatory requirements when it comes to content, e.g. that a Decision includes reasons, in our view it is likely that the substance and content of a Decision is more important than its form.

In broad terms we would expect a Decision to have a title page, a section setting out the procedural history of the adjudication, a section setting out the adjudicator's consideration of the substantive dispute (including their reasons), and a final section summarizing the Decision. This final section is sometimes referred to as the 'dispositive' section of the Decision, i.e. it is disposing of the matter referred and telling people what the Decision is and what to do by when.

Irrespective of the structure or format adopted, our view is that a Decision should be well presented and come across as a well-prepared and professional document. A good first impression can only be a good thing. Conversely, a poorly prepared or badly presented document will not create a positive initial view, and it could also distract the reader from the important content and potentially irritate them too – none of this will serve the adjudicator well. Simple things such as numbering the pages and including paragraph numbers can therefore be important in this regard. These things can also serve a practical purpose in terms of navigating the Decision and referencing it, either as part of the Decision itself or by the parties, a judge or a subsequent adjudicator. This will also make identification of slips or errors and administration of any corrections easier.

Title page

Again, while there is no prescribed format for the title page of a Decision, by convention they tend to follow the format of an arbitration award. Thinking about the purpose of a title page helps elucidate what it should include. As with a book, you should expect to be able to identify what the document is by looking at its cover.

The rubric 'In the matter of an adjudication' is typically used at the top of the page, either on its own or sometimes expanded to include a reference to the applicable statute, contract or adjudication provisions. Thereafter, we would expect to see the parties' names and the title of the document itself, the name of the adjudicator, and the date of the

Decision. When naming the parties, we would expect the full name of the legal entity to be included along with an indication of whether they were the party referring the dispute to adjudication or the party responding. Conventionally the parties will be known as the Referring Party and the Responding Party, but we have also seen them referred to as the applicant/claimant and the respondent.

In addition to denoting in the title that the document is an 'Adjudicator's Decision', it may also be helpful to include an additional identifying reference (or references), especially if there have already been previous adjudications. This may take the form of a number, e.g. 'Adjudication No 2', or by reference to the dispute, e.g. 'Variation No 2', 'Extension of Time Claim No 1', etc. Similarly, it might be the case that there are a number of adjudications between the same parties but in respect of different contracts, such that it might also be helpful to refer to the project or contract itself. Including a footer with a reference – again to help identify the Decision or distinguish it from other Decisions involving the same parties on the same or separate contracts – may also be beneficial.

We have included an example Decision in appendix B, and we hope readers will find it helpful to see examples of sections of a Decision as the chapter progresses.

Contents

The question of whether to include a contents page will again be a matter of personal choice, but they can undoubtedly be helpful in assisting the reader in navigating the document, particularly if sections are hyperlinked so that the reader can quickly go to the section they are interested in. To a certain extent the act of creating a contents page can also assist with structuring the Decision itself, to ensure it flows in a logical sequence.

In broad terms we consider that there are typically three main sections to a Decision. The first section is what we refer to as the 'preamble'. This is where the procedural history of the adjudication is set out. The second section is what we refer to as the 'substantive' part of the Decision. This is where the adjudicator addresses the substantive dispute in question and determines the issues and matters that fall to be decided. It should also include the adjudicator's reasons. The final section is what we refer to as either the 'operative' or 'dispositive' part of the Decision. Here, the adjudicator sets out in clear terms the declarations and decisions that dispose of the matter referred. The preamble and the substantive part of the Decision are likely to be broken down into a number of subsections.

Preamble

The purpose of the preamble section is to set out the procedural history of the adjudication. It should set out how the adjudicator came to be appointed, the details of the underlying contract and applicable procedural rules, the nature of the dispute referred, and the procedure adopted. It should also set out details of the representatives; the submissions and evidence received; any meeting, hearing or site inspection; the redress that is sought; and any significant procedural correspondence, together with objections to the appointment and any jurisdictional challenges and decisions made in that respect.

The appointment

The appointment section should provide a record of how the adjudicator was appointed, including details of whether the appointment was the result of a nomination, of an agreement between the parties, or of the fact that the adjudicator was named in the contract. Including relevant dates can be helpful.

This section should also include details of the parties. When mentioning the parties for the first time, we consider it appropriate to give their names in full (perhaps with the relevant company numbers if the company name has different translations, as is the case between Arabic and English, for example), but to use a shortened name or acronym thereafter. By convention, the abbreviated names are included in brackets and within speech marks to denote a 'defined' term for the purpose of the Decision. While some adjudicators refer to the parties as the Referring Party and the Responding Party within their Decisions, in our view this increases the potential for getting the parties mixed up. This could apply equally to acronyms that include the same letters, so some thought should be given to what abbreviations are used. If the parties have used the same shortened names or acronyms, it is often simplest to use these for consistency. An alternative is to use the terms in the underlying contract, e.g. 'Employer' or 'Contractor', and we have done this where the employer is a private individual or comprises partners in a dispute concerning a private residence.

There should also be reference to the underlying contract, the project and the applicable adjudication provisions. Where there is no issue between the parties in these respects this should be a relatively straightforward task, but sometimes the parties do not agree as to the applicable terms, the formation of the contract or the procedural rules. In such circumstances we would suggest recording the fact of any disagreement and also a reference or signpost to how or where that matter is dealt with within the Decision – assuming it is necessary to determine the issue. If nothing turns on the disagreement, this fact should also be recorded. For example, it may be that the disagreement regarding the precise terms of the contract does not affect the right to adjudicate or the specific dispute that has been referred.

Summary of the dispute

We believe there should be a description of the dispute that has been referred. This could simply be a case of including the description of the dispute that is included in a Notice of Adjudication, and we have seen examples where the description is included as a screenshot extract or copied and pasted into the Decision in italics. This may well be appropriate when the description included in a Notice is relatively short, but we sometimes find it can run to several pages, with extensive reference to the background to the dispute. In such circumstances, our view is that it is preferable to summarize the dispute at a high level instead of including it in full. The upper limit in terms of length should be one page – and this should not be treated as a target to aim for!

In terms of the content of the summary of the dispute, it should include the positions of both parties. Although a dispute will, by definition, require there to be a disagreement (either express or implied) – and the description of the dispute in a Notice or Referral should therefore at the very least record the fact that a claim has not been admitted or has been expressly rejected – the reasons for the disagreement or the detail of the Responding Party's position may not be fully articulated until the Response is served. If that is the case, it might also be necessary to refer to the content of the Response in order to set out the position of the Responding Party and also to the Reply in order to include any responsive position of the Referring Party.

As the adjudication progresses, it may be that new issues arise and/or that concessions are made such that the dispute that was originally referred evolves or changes. For this reason we recommend that the section that sets out a summary of the dispute should be kept under review – it is surprising how much of our summaries can sometimes seem irrelevant when they are reviewed on the completion of the Decision. Although we understand the need (or, at least, the temptation) to draft sections of the Decision as and when submissions are received, we do not consider it helpful for a Decision to include extensive 'cut and paste' or 'he said/she said'-type recitations of the Referral, the Response, the Reply, the Rejoinder, etc., especially if an issue is ultimately settled or redundant on account of a concession or of common ground being found. Therefore, even if an adjudicator elects to draft as and when the submissions are served and read, we recommend adopting a critical eye during the final drafting stage in order to avoid any unnecessary or superfluous content.

The procedure

This should be a relatively straightforward section to draft. If there has been no reference to the parties' representatives within any earlier sections (e.g. in the introduction or the appointment section), then we would mention them here. We would also record whether counsel have been instructed. Assuming they have been helpful, we would thank the parties' representatives and/or counsel where appropriate for their cooperation or assistance.

This section should also include a list of the submissions received and the dates when they were served. We would also include here a list of any witness statements and experts who have prepared reports. While we have seen more extensive records of the correspondence received recited in Decisions, we believe a balance needs to be struck between recording the essential submissions received and the additional time and expense of recording *all* of the supporting documents and appendices received. That said, if the documents received in correspondence are particularly voluminous or extensive, it can be helpful to highlight this fact.

Where there has been a meeting, hearing or site inspection, details should be included, with a record of when and where it (or they) took place and who was in attendance. If additional documents were received at the meeting, they can be recorded too.

We would also record whether reasons have been requested or are required. We do have experience of parties expressly asking for no reasons, but this is rare, and in the vast majority of instances the parties request reasons and/or reasons are relevant under the relevant contract or adjudication rules. Even if the parties have made no mention of reasons, we would normally provide them to assist the parties in understanding the Decision, as well as to assist us in reaching findings on the issues, as we discuss further below.

Finally, assuming that the date by which the Decision is to be reached has not already been recorded in an earlier section, we would do that here. We would also record whether the date was set as a result of a timetable prescribed by legislation, procedural rules or the contract, or alternatively whether it was set following one or both parties agreeing to extend the date for the Decision.

Matters to be decided

The matters to be decided constitute the issues that fall to be determined in order to decide whether or not to grant the redress sought. We consider it important that the redress sought is set out in full, either by cutting and pasting (or quoting) – in whole or in part – from the substantive submissions. However, the adjudicator might wish to redraft the redress so that it reads in the first person. If this approach is taken, it might be helpful to identify any words that have been substituted by including square brackets around them, e.g. 'X seeks an order that [my] fees and expenses are paid by Y'.

Having set out the redress sought, we consider it good practice to then set out the substantive issues in the order in which the adjudicator has elected to address them. The issues will then form the subsections of the substantive part of the Decision.

Jurisdiction

If there has been a challenge to the adjudicator's threshold jurisdiction or an issue regarding the adjudicator's internal jurisdiction, this should be recorded within the Decision. We understand that some adjudicators choose to record when there have been no jurisdictional issues raised, but we do not adopt this approach ourselves. Doing so does, at the very least, highlight to the reader that no challenge was made, and this may be relevant should a party wish to raise a point at a later date.

If there has been a jurisdictional challenge or issue and this was dealt with during the course of the adjudication, then the procedure adopted and the conclusion should be set out within the body of the Decision. Although some adjudicators may wish to refer to or append correspondence that sets out any conclusion or explanation provided, we tend to quote the relevant sections of such correspondence within the Decision. This enables the reader to understand the reasons for the adjudicator's conclusion. We also consider it good practice to record whether a party's continued participation in the adjudication after the conclusion was communicated was subject to any reservation of its position.

It might sometimes be the case that the adjudicator did not have time to set out their reasons for concluding that they had jurisdiction when the challenge was made. In such circumstances, the Decision will give the adjudicator the opportunity to provide their reasons. Similarly, where the adjudicator has elected to address (for example) an internal jurisdictional issue within their Decision, it will be necessary to set out the adjudicator's conclusion on the issue and their reasons.

The substantive part of the Decision

The content of the substantive part of the Decision will be determined by the issues as formulated by the adjudicator. Likewise, the order in which the adjudicator has elected to address the issues will determine the structure. Each issue will therefore form a subsection of the substantive part of the Decision. Within each subsection we would expect to see a summary of the parties' positions on the issue that requires determination, a recitation of relevant facts, references to the applicable provisions of the contract or law that the parties have referred to, the adjudicator's analysis of and conclusion on the disputed facts and/or law, and their reasons for reaching their conclusion.

Setting out the parties' positions

The extent to which it is necessary to set out the parties' positions within the substantive part of the Decision will depend on whether the positions have already been set out within the preamble, and in particular in the section summarizing the dispute. If the positions have already been set out in detail, it is not necessary to repeat them, but if they have only been set out in summary form, as is likely, they should be set out in sufficient detail in this part of the Decision to demonstrate to the parties that the adjudicator has understood their positions and also to enable the uninvolved reader to understand those positions.

We do not advocate the practice of extensive cutting and pasting of the parties' positions or recitation of the content of each round of submissions. In our view a summary of the parties' positions is sufficient, together with reference to any evidence or legal authority relied on in support of their positions.

Recitation of relevant facts or references to applicable provisions of the contract or law

An issue will ultimately be determined by a combination of the adjudicator reaching a decision on any disputed fact or law and, thereafter, an application of the law (as decided or agreed) to the facts (as decided or agreed). It is therefore helpful for the Decision to include references to facts (including any common ground) that will be relevant to the adjudicator's analysis; this might include quotations from correspondence or contemporaneous documents. Similarly, it may be useful for the Decision to include relevant extracts from the contract or legislation.

Determining the law

Where the law or a legal principle is not agreed, the adjudicator will need to determine the position to be adopted and include reasons as to why the adjudicator has reached their conclusion. It is important to remember that the adjudicator's task is to decide on the legal arguments advanced by the parties. Therefore, if the adjudicator believes that a legal point that has not been raised by either party is relevant to the matter in hand, they will either need to raise that with the parties and invite comments or not take the legal point in question into account.

Having received the parties' submissions on the law, the adjudicator will need to explain which position they prefer and why they prefer it. This might be a simple matter of accepting that one party's interpretation is correct based on the authorities, or it might require a more detailed analysis of the authorities. In either case, what is important is that the adjudicator sets out the conclusion on the legal issue in clear terms so that it can then be applied to the facts.

Assessing evidence

Where facts are in issue the adjudicator will need to determine which factual position is to be preferred. The applicable standard is the civil standard, i.e. on the balance of probabilities. The fact therefore needs to be deemed to be more likely than not to be true. Some asserted facts may be accepted on the basis of an explanation provided if said explanation is deemed to be credible by virtue of being within a reasonable range of expectation. Others might require an assessment of documents, correspondence, photographs, videos or expert opinion evidence in order to reach a conclusion as to whether it is more likely than not to have occurred. It is difficult to be prescriptive as to what will be required in order to discharge the evidential burden, and what is sufficient to persuade one adjudicator might be different to what is required to persuade another. What is important is that the adjudicator is alive to which party is required to make out its case in demonstrating a particular fact; ordinarily, it will be the party making or advancing a claim.

Where expert evidence is involved, the same principles will apply regarding the burden of proof. Although an expert's evidence should, strictly speaking, be restricted to their opinion, in some instances an expert may be instructed to collate or present factual information. In our experience this is often the case with experts who have been tasked with opining on delay, and it can often be helpful.

Although the civil standard of proof is on the balance of probabilities, where allegations of dishonesty or fraud are made, more evidence may be required due to the seriousness of the allegations. For a finding of fraud or dishonesty to be made, therefore, the evidence in support of an allegation will need to be compelling.

Deciding the dispute: how?

An adjudicator's role is to make decisions about matters that are not agreed between the parties. Those matters will typically involve factual and/or legal matters. In the context of a contractual dispute, the adjudicator will need to determine any disputed fact based on their assessment of the evidence; they will need to reach a decision as to what the applicable law, legal principle or provision of the contract means; and they will then have to apply the facts (as found or agreed) to the law (again as found or agreed) in order to reach a conclusion. In simple terms, it could be (and sometimes is) described as the determination of disputed (or agreed) fact + the determination of disputed (or agreed) law = decision. Although some issues do not obviously lend themselves to the adoption of such a simple formula, in essence this is what is required in order for an adjudicator to reach a decision.

Artificial intelligence

Although it is a relatively recent phenomenon, the subject of artificial intelligence (AI) is increasingly being discussed in the field of dispute resolution. We are aware that certain jurisdictions are already adopting the use of AI to reach decisions in respect of low-value claims or for certain types of issue, e.g. disputed parking fines and the like. However, it needs to be remembered that it is the adjudicator who is tasked with reaching a Decision, and therefore any delegation of the decision-making function would be inappropriate unless the parties agree to adopting such a procedure. It may be that the parties agree to the use of AI to assist with a sampling exercise, e.g. in order to identify an appropriate sample and/or apply the findings in respect of a sample to a wider data set. The key here is transparency, so it would be highly inappropriate for an adjudicator to use AI without disclosing their intention to do so and obtaining consent if appropriate.

Reasons

Although we are aware that an adjudicator will not always be obliged to give reasons, in our experience this is not the norm. Adjudicators will almost invariably be required to give reasons for their Decision, and even if they are not, we believe that the process of writing reasons can assist in the decision-making process and is therefore good practice. On more than one occasion we have reached what we thought was a conclusion on an issue only to hit a stumbling block when it comes to writing the reasons. In such circumstances it can often be helpful to list the reasons both for and against a particular conclusion because, in our experience, this can provide clarity as to whether the original conclusion was correct or if it needs to be changed.

How reasons are presented will again vary depending on individual style or preference. While some adjudicators prefer a descriptive commentary, in longer, flowing paragraphs, others prefer to set out reasons in a list form: for example, 'I find that the correct value of the prolongation costs is $500,000 because …', followed by subparagraphs each setting out an individual reason. What is important is that the reader (and especially the losing party) understands why the adjudicator has decided in the way that they have. In some instances it may be as simple as saying that the adjudicator prefers the evidence or submission of one party over that of the other, but that is only likely to be appropriate where there are multiple line items in dispute and/or where the amount in dispute is low. Such reasoning will be insufficient in most cases as the reader will not understand why the adjudicator preferred the evidence or submission. We therefore recommend that an adjudicator adopts a critical eye when reviewing or setting out their reasons for a particular finding. There may be multiple reasons for a given finding, or it could simply be the case that the adjudicator considers the evidence to be consistent with a contemporaneous document or just more credible. One tip when reviewing a draft is to ask whether the reasons given might lead the reader to question why a particular finding has been made. We refer to this as the 'Why test'. If a supposed reason fails the 'Why test', it is likely to be the case that further explanation is required.

The reason for a finding may sometimes be because the adjudicator is not persuaded that an allegation or statement of facts is made out. This may be a result of insufficient supporting evidence being provided, or it might be a consequence of evidence or submissions to the contrary. Again, the key point here is that the adjudicator must explain why they are not persuaded. It may also be helpful for the adjudicator to explain the applicable evidential principles, including who has the evidential burden in respect of an alleged fact or set of circumstances. It should be noted, though, that it will rarely be appropriate, in our view, for an adjudicator to simply state that they adopt a party's case because the other party has not discharged their burden of proof; such an unreasoned finding is likely to fail the 'Why test'.

Schedules/appendices/tables

Where there are a large numbers of items in dispute – such as a variation account, or claims for defects or other deductions – it may be appropriate for the adjudicator to set out their findings and reasons in a schedule appended to the main body of the Decision.[1] There are no hard and fast rules as to when the use of schedules as an appendix is appropriate, but a useful guide is to consider whether the incorporation of reasons and/or findings within the main body of a Decision would make the Decision unwieldy or difficult to navigate. Where the parties have themselves either provided or used schedules setting out their positions and have included columns for the adjudicator to set out findings and comments (or reasons), this might give an indication that a schedule appended to the Decision is appropriate.

Where schedules are appended, it may be that the adjudicator elects to set out a more detailed explanation of the approach that they have adopted or of the reasons for their findings in respect of recurring issues within the main body of their Decision, e.g. the applicable valuation rules or rate(s) that should apply. The schedule could then contain a shorter and/or abbreviated comment that could also be cross-referenced to the main body of the Decision.

It should also be made clear that any schedule appended to the Decision still nevertheless forms part of the substantive Decision itself. The adjudicator should put some thought into the format of the schedule and take care not to include anything that they would not wish to

---

1 We also discussed schedules in chapter 7, and we have included an example of a schedule dealing with variations in appendix C.

communicate. If the schedule is provided as a PDF, this is unlikely to be an issue; but if the schedule is provided in its native format, e.g. Excel, more care will be needed. For example, if the adjudicator has used a schedule prepared by the parties as a working document that includes the parties' comments, these should be removed or suitably redacted unless the adjudicator is happy for the content to be disclosed as part of their Decision.

Party costs

An important part of the adjudicator's Decision will be the determination of who should pay the costs of the adjudication and/or the fees of the adjudicator. Although in most jurisdictions the convention is that the parties will bear their own costs, this is not universal and it may be that the adjudicator is required to reach a Decision on costs. Likewise, although most jurisdictions allow the adjudicator to determine who should pay their fees, in some instances the legislation or contract may prescribe how the adjudicator's fees are to be paid.

Where the adjudicator is required to determine the parties' costs, they will need to consider what procedure to adopt. In contrast to litigation and arbitration, the adjudicator will typically be required to reach their Decision by a certain date set down in legislation, contract or the procedural rules. In litigation or arbitration it is usual for the determination of the substantive dispute or claim to be addressed separately from costs. The parties will therefore be aware of the outcome of the underlying claim, and their submissions on costs will be made in the knowledge of the result of the proceedings. This will not be the case in adjudication unless the parties agree that the adjudicator is to reach separate Decisions. In principle, there is nothing wrong with such an approach so long as both parties agree to it. In such circumstances, the adjudicator can seek agreement and, if it is obtained, set out directions for a procedure whereby the parties can make their submissions and/or provide details of their costs to enable the adjudicator to reach a separate Decision on costs.

Where the adjudicator is given the power to determine party costs but the parties have not agreed to a separate Decision, the adjudicator will need to invite the parties to provide details of their costs along with any submissions or comments on those costs. Thereafter, how the adjudicator reaches their Decision on costs will not differ materially to the position where a separate Decision on costs is provided, save that there could be a logistical issue that arises in the event of the adjudicator being asked to consider any offers that have been made. No such issue should arise where there is a separate Decision on costs, but where there is a single Decision the adjudicator will need to consider how any offers are dealt with as it would be inappropriate for the content of any offers to be known prior to the adjudicator reaching their Decision on the underlying substantive dispute. This could compromise the adjudicator's position and result in an allegation of a perception of bias or a breach of natural justice. In order to overcome this, we suggest that the adjudicator adopts a procedure whereby they reach their findings on the substantive dispute, communicate that they have done so, and then proceed to address costs – including any offers that they have been made aware of.

Although the approach to addressing costs may differ between jurisdictions, conventionally the approach to adopt is that the 'winning' party will be awarded their reasonable costs and the 'losing' party will pay those costs as well as their own. This is referred to as the 'costs follow the event' principle, whereby the event is the outcome of the dispute resolution process and – unless there are good grounds for departing from the principle – the winner should get their reasonable costs. Examples of grounds for departing from the principle include if the conduct of the winner was such that it unnecessarily increased the costs of the process, say, or if the amount recovered was modest in the context of the amount claimed, or if there had been an offer that was not beaten. Further, it may be that there were a number of issues or matters upon which both parties had some success.

The first question is, therefore: who was the 'winner'? If a party was awarded all of the amount claimed, the answer will be clear-cut and it will then be a case of considering whether there was conduct or circumstances that mean that it is inappropriate for that party to be awarded all or part of their reasonable costs. If an offer has been made, the question of whether a party has won will need to be considered in the context of whether the offer was beaten or not. If there has been neither poor conduct nor an offer that affects the outcome, such that there is a clear winner, then it is a matter of considering whether the costs claimed are reasonable. This will also depend on the facts and may involve considering whether the number of individuals involved was reasonable, as well as their level of experience and their charge-out rates.

Where there is no clear-cut winner and/or there are circumstances that justify a departure from the 'costs follow the event' principle, it may be appropriate to limit or apportion costs recovery. This could involve a finding that both parties bear their own costs, or perhaps the costs recovery will be determined by reducing one party's costs to reflect a split award. Where there has been an offer during the course of the adjudication, the timing may also be relevant: costs before and after the time at which an offer was open for acceptance fall to be allocated differently.

The adjudicator's fees and expenses

The principles that apply to the determination of liability for the adjudicator's fees are similar to those that apply to the determination of liability for party costs except that, conventionally, it would be unusual to have separate Decisions dealing with the substantive dispute and liability for fees. That said, if there have been offers, it may be that the parties agree to such an approach to avoid any complications on account of the adjudicator being privy to privileged or without-prejudice material. Ordinarily, the adjudicator will therefore be required to address liability for their fees within their Decision.

Unless the legislation or the contract prescribes that the fees are paid in a certain way, the adjudicator is likely to be given discretion over who should pay their fees. Where that is the case, the adjudicator will typically adopt the 'costs follow the event' approach described above. However, there is often no clear-cut 'winner', and where both parties have enjoyed a level of success it may be appropriate for the adjudicator to assess their fees on the basis of the time spent on matters for which the parties have been successful. The adjudicator may also take into account any increased time spent on tasks that may have been unnecessary but for poor conduct, the making of bad points, poor presentation, repetitive submissions, etc. In order to undertake such an assessment, it will be necessary for the adjudicator to have kept a record of their time spent on significant tasks, or at the very least to have allocated their costs to the various functions undertaken, e.g. appointment, administration, general correspondence, the drafting of the preamble, time spent reviewing the various submissions or addressing distinct issues, general drafting and undertaking a final review. Professional timesheet software is very useful for this purpose. Indeed, we consider it to be an essential tool for an adjudicator.

A key point to note is that any decision on costs or fees will represent an integral part of the adjudicator's Decision. Thus, to the extent the adjudicator is required to provide reasons, they will also need to explain why they have reached their decision in respect of costs or fees. This may therefore require an explanation of the applicable principles, their conclusion on who has 'won', and why they consider it appropriate for any apportionment and/or why they applied a particular apportionment.

The dispositive section/the conclusion

This section represents the operative part of the Decision. it is where the adjudicator will set out their decision including any declarations or orders. It is important that this part of the Decision makes clear what has been decided and unambiguously sets out who is to do what and, if applicable, by when.

It is important that the adjudicator addresses all of the matters referred and the redress sought by the parties that falls within their jurisdiction or the scope of the adjudication. A good starting point is to check the redress sought and to make sure that each element is covered. We are aware that some adjudicators will set out the redress verbatim, followed by a comment: 'Granted', 'Declined', and so on. This can work where the decision either reflects the redress sought unamended or where the answer to the redress sought is a binary yes or no, but where this is not the position, it may be better for the adjudicator to formulate wording that reflects their findings by reference to each element of the redress sought.

In relation to the time for performance, in most instances the parties will have included a time period in their redress, e.g. payment within seven days, immediately or forthwith. Where this is the case, we would suggest adopting that time period (subject to any amendment thought necessary as a result of opposing submission or argument). The word 'forthwith' is arguably not specific, although lawyers would understand the term to mean as soon as is practicable or reasonable. Where no time period is sought, we consider it to be good practice for the adjudicator to specify a period.

If interest is awarded, we believe it is sensible to calculate the amount of interest up to the date of the Decision and to specify any continuing interest that will apply between the date of the Decision and the date when payment is made. We tend to specify a daily amount, but this may not be appropriate if only part payment is made against the Decision. In that case it might be better to specify a rate or a type of interest to account for that.

The adjudicator will also need to set out their decision on their fees and expenses, including directions on how payment of their fees is to be effected. Although some adjudicators include the amount of their fees within their Decision, not all do. In any event, they will still need to specify who is liable, including details of any apportionment. Where there has been, the applicable percentages and/or amounts should be included. We also consider it sensible to include a reference to the fact that the parties remain joint and severally liable for payment of the fees notwithstanding any findings on primary liability. For this reason, it is also useful for the adjudicator to include wording to the effect that, if one party pays fees that have been ordered to be paid by the other party, they should be reimbursed.

Although it is not a practice that we generally adopt, we are aware that some adjudicators will order one party – typically the Referring Party – to pay in the first instance irrespective of whether they have been successful, either in whole or in part. Our understanding of the rationale for this is that if the Referring Party is awarded sums and the other party is found liable for the adjudicator's fees, the Referring Party can then recover any fees paid from the other party either as a result of voluntary compliance with the Decision or as part of any formal recovery proceedings. This approach would therefore offer some protection to the adjudicator in the event the Responding Party did not comply with the adjudicator's Decision.

One school of thought is that requiring payment from one party regardless of the result could lead to a perception of bias, although we are not aware of this argument being successful in any past enforcement proceedings. The counter argument is that it is the Referring Party who has elected to refer the dispute to adjudication with the understanding that they are joint and severally liable for the adjudicator's fees, and therefore, the argument goes, it is entirely reasonable for them to be asked to pay the adjudicator's fees in the first instance and to pursue the other party if applicable.

It may also be the case that the adjudicator is permitted to exercise a lien on release of their Decision pending payment of their fees, and/or that they are entitled to obtain payment on account in advance of their Decision. If this is permitted, the Decision will also need to include appropriate words to put effect to the ultimate decision on liability and to provide for any reimbursement where advance payment has been made.

However, where an adjudicator has attempted to exercise a lien or has required payment but either one or both parties have not made payment, the adjudicator will need to consider whether it is possible and/or appropriate for them to withhold release of their Decision. Where it is possible to exercise a lien, the adjudicator will need to consider whether they still wish to hold onto their Decision as this may preclude them from formally pursing payment. Additionally, where case law, legislation and/or the applicable adjudication rules do not permit liens (such as in the United Kingdom), the adjudicator may well lose the right to any payment at all on account of a failure to reach and publish their Decision within the prescribed timescale.

WHEN SHOULD THE ADJUDICATOR START DRAFTING?

In view of the time-limited nature of adjudication it is understandable that an adjudicator might wish to start drafting their Decision as early as possible. In terms of the preamble, there is no reason why the appointment section and the details of the contract and applicable adjudication provisions cannot be drafted soon after the Referral is served. Similarly, once the Response is served it might be possible to include details of the dispute and the parties' respective positions, but it is important to keep any early drafting under review and to be sure to account for any amendments to the parties' positions or procedural developments that manifest themselves during the course of the adjudication.

Although it may not be possible to proceed with the decision-making process until submissions are finally closed, it may be possible to proceed with some elements of the decision making where submissions on certain issues are complete (assuming that those issues precede issues where submissions are still ongoing). Where this occurs, it might be the case that the drafting in respect of the substantive parts of the Decision on those issues can proceed at an earlier stage. However, even where submissions are ongoing, it may be that some drafting can commence as soon as the issues have been formulated. This is typically after the

Response is served, and the drafting can then be refined as and when further submissions are provided. In particular, it may be possible to draft the sections of the substantive Decision setting out the parties' positions, to set out headings or sections where the adjudicator's findings or conclusions can be included at a later date, and so on. Likewise, relevant sections of the contract may also be set out if it is likely that they will require analysis or referencing.

Where the adjudicator elects to set out the parties' positions at an early stage, these will again need to be kept under review. We have already mentioned that we do not advocate an extensive recitation of the parties' positions in a sequential way, e.g. 'In the Referral X said …', 'in the Response Y said …', 'in the Reply X said …', 'in the Rejoinder Y said …', 'in the Surrejoinder X conceded the point', etc. Although an adjudicator may wish to summarize the submissions as and when they are received, our view is that ultimately these should be condensed so that they reflect the final position.

Once the submissions are closed (either on an issue or in full), the adjudicator will be able to proceed with the decision-making process. This will involve an analysis of the submissions, the evidence, the contract and the applicable law, and it will require the adjudicator to reach their conclusion on each issue and subissue. Some adjudicators might wish to conclude their decision on every aspect of the dispute before drafting. Others might wish to proceed sequentially through each issue, i.e. once they reach a conclusion on an issue they then draft that section of their Decision. The advantage of the latter approach is that the drafting can be progressed earlier, which might assist with any proofing that is required. The disadvantage is that the adjudicator might need to revise or amend earlier sections of their Decision as a result of later findings or discoveries. However, as decision making is an iterative process and the Decision is not concluded until it is published, there is nothing inherently wrong with this, and it may actually result in a more robust decision as a result of keeping earlier 'decisions' under review and ensuring consistency.

PROOFING/PRODUCTION

It is important to allow adequate time for proofing and formatting the Decision (including any accompanying schedules). In our view, proofing by another person – a 'second pair of eyes' so to speak – is preferable, but we understand that this may not be possible. Although using someone to proofread may raise confidentiality issues, in our experience this is not an issue and can be covered in an adjudicator's terms. We also find it useful to have someone undertake a clerical or arithmetical check to ensure that calculations are correct and that the correct numbers are carried through from the individual paragraphs into any tables, etc. It is important to note, however, that the proofing process should not alter the adjudicator's substantive findings, unless that alteration results from a clerical error or omission identified during the proofing. It could otherwise be argued that the Decision is not the product of the adjudicator's own work.

Where an adjudicator tasks someone with proofing and clerical checks, this will need to be planned and coordinated, i.e. when will the Decision (or parts of it) be sent for proofing and when will it (or they) be returned? Thereafter, the adjudicator will need to allow time to administer any corrections and undertake a final review. One technique that we are aware of (as part of either an initial proofread or a final review) is to make time for the adjudicator to actually read the Decision out loud or to use word processing software to read it out loud so they can listen to it, e.g. using text to speech functionality. In our experience this is more likely to identify any errors than merely reading the Decision. This is on the basis that we tend to read what we think we have written as opposed to what we have actually written.

CHAPTER 10

Post Decision

There might still be work for the adjudicator to do after the Decision is published. The most obvious function to perform post Decision is to attend to any necessary corrections, but that might not be the only matter that the adjudicator is involved with and/or that the adjudicator needs to consider in connection with the Decision and their role. This chapter covers these aspects of the role of the adjudicator.

SLIPS/ERRORS

The power to make corrections will usually arise as a result of an express provision in the relevant legislation, the adjudication procedural rules and/or the contract, but it could also arise as a result of decided case law. Although the scope of the power may vary, in broad terms it is typically restricted to 'slips or errors'. This then leads to the question of what constitutes a slip or error?

In simple terms, a slip or error will represent an unintended arithmetical, clerical or typographical mistake. In most instances these will be obvious, but sometimes an unintended slip might not be so obvious and may only manifest itself as a result of an inconsistency or when the adjudicator reviews their Decision and realizes that what was written down did not reflect their intentions.

A key principle behind what is referred to as 'the slip rule' is that an adjudicator should be given the opportunity to correct mistakes within their Decision so that it reflects their intentions. Another key principle is that the slip rule is not an opportunity for the adjudicator to change their Decision on account of having second thoughts or as a result of a further submission. With these principles in mind it should be relatively obvious (at least to the adjudicator) whether or not their Decision contains an error that falls within the ambit of the slip rule.

Errors can be identified either by the parties or by the adjudicator. The time for corrections of errors may be prescribed. If it is not, it may be that the time is limited by implication, e.g. within a 'reasonable' time. In the event an error is identified after the time period prescribed (or is not within whatever a 'reasonable' period is deemed to be), then the adjudicator will arguably not have the power to correct it unless the parties agree. If it is the adjudicator who discovers an error after the time period prescribed, then they might choose not to raise it with the parties, but if an error is identified by a party, then, assuming the adjudicator accepts that it is a genuine error within the scope of the slip rule, our view is that the adjudicator should ask the parties to confirm whether they are happy for a correction to be administered. If both parties agree, then we see no good reason not to correct the Decision, but if they do not, there is unlikely to be any power for the adjudicator to make the correction. This then leads to the question of whether there is any purpose in the adjudicator confirming that they accept there is an error. On the one hand, doing so may obviate any further argument and/or the need for a further reference to adjudication or the commencement of proceedings before another tribunal. On the other hand, the adjudicator's confirmation of an error has no status and will not alter the Decision. There could also be unintended consequences, and, therefore, no matter how well intended the adjudicator might be, our view is that the most prudent course of action would be to refrain from commenting. We accept, however, that others might adopt a different course of action on the basis that it may be unconscionable for them not to admit that there was an error.

Assuming that there is no issue of being timed out, then the approach adopted for dealing with any errors will depend on whether the error is identified by the adjudicator or by the parties. If the adjudicator spots the error, then it is normally just a matter of them advising the parties and publishing a corrected Decision. If it is a party who identifies what it considers to be an error, though, then the adjudicator's first task will be to consider whether the matter(s) identified do represent an error within the scope of the slip rule as a matter of fact. If so, the adjudicator should acknowledge the point and (if considered appropriate) administer the correction(s). Conversely, if the adjudicator does not accept that the matter identified is an error, then they should communicate that to the parties and decline any request to 'correct' or amend their Decision.

In some instances, the question of whether a matter identified is an error within the scope of the slip rule may not be clear to the adjudicator. In such circumstances, and if time permits, the adjudicator could invite comment from the other party (assuming that they have not already provided it that is: in our experience parties are quick to respond to any request to 'correct' if they do not accept that the matter identified is an error within the scope of the slip rule!). As well as actually providing some assistance to the adjudicator regarding the question of whether the matter constitutes a slip, it may also give the adjudicator more time (assuming it is available), which may in itself be helpful. Thereafter, the adjudicator will then have to decide whether the matter identified is an error that they have power to correct. If the conclusion is that they do not, then this needs to be communicated. In our view, a short explanation as to why the matter is not considered to be a slip is appropriate. This could be no more than confirming that the Decision reflects their intention.

If the adjudicator concludes that there is an error, the adjudicator will then need to confirm as much and also confirm what the corrections are. This can take a number of forms, and the easiest will be to set out corrections in correspondence. The adjudicator could instead issue an 'erratum' in the form of a standalone document. Finally, the adjudicator could issue a corrected Decision; unless the parties agree otherwise, this is our preference.

An ancillary consideration when administering corrections is whether there is a consequential effect of the corrections on the result and on other parts of the Decision. If there is, the adjudicator should administer the consequential corrections. If this means that the previously declared 'winner' is now the 'loser', such that the element of the Decision dealing with costs or fees needs amendment, then that should be addressed. Although this may be embarrassing for the adjudicator, our view is that it is important that the Decision reflects the adjudicator's intent and is therefore logically 'correct' and consistent.

RELEVANT CASE LAW

The UK case of *Axis M&E UK Ltd & Anor v Multiplex Construction Europe Ltd*[1] is an apt example of consequential corrections to a Decision.

Axis, an M&E subcontractor employed by a main contractor, Multiplex, referred a dispute to adjudication regarding the value of its works and the sum due to it, and the dispute also included Multiplex's entitlement to deduct contra-charges.

In the adjudicator's original Decision, he concluded that Axis's claim failed as he found there was a negative balance due to it. As the claim failed, there was no entitlement to interest and the adjudicator's fees and expenses were Axis's responsibility. Four days later, the adjudicator issued a corrected Decision and, this time, he found that Axis was entitled to £654,000 plus interest. The adjudicator also decided that Multiplex was liable for his fees and expenses. He reached these conclusions after being told of an error with the contra-charges, which he had effectively taken into account twice.

When it came to the enforcement proceedings that followed the corrected Decision, Multiplex argued that the adjudicator did not have jurisdiction to make the changes he had included in his corrected Decision because they went beyond those permitted by paragraph 22A of the Scheme for Construction Contracts 1998. The judge disagreed with Multiplex and concluded that the adjudicator did have jurisdiction to make the changes because, 'once one element of a decision has been corrected, then any other changes consequential upon that correction should be made, since otherwise the decision is likely to be internally inconsistent'.

In terms of communication of the corrected Decision, we would recommend that the adjudicator produces a 'tracked changes' document that shows the original text struck out and the replacement text highlighted. We also consider it helpful to expressly state that the Decision is 'corrected' and to make the date of the correction clear. This may require a note on the title page, the signature page and also an amended footer. It may also be helpful in any covering communication to record

1 [2019] EWHC 169 (TCC).

which paragraphs or sections have been corrected, meaning the parties will not need to reread unamended sections.

We are also aware of situations in which, having issued a corrected Decision, further errors are identified. These would then also fall to be corrected and a 're-corrected' Decision (or even a 're-re-corrected Decision') issued in the same way as the corrected Decision.

Although embarrassing for the adjudicator, the fact is that adjudicators are human (at least for now!). It is therefore inevitable that slips and errors will occasionally occur. This is especially so in a time-limited process that does not allow for the 'luxury' of being able to circulate a draft judgment or award to facilitate the identification of such slips by the parties. That said, we are aware of at least one adjudicator who has actually adopted this approach, where the time pressures were deemed to be subordinate to the parties' desire for a 'correct' Decision. In time this may become more widespread for complex adjudications, although readers should note our comments in chapter 7 on the risks involved with draft Decisions.

A final point here relates to the question of whether an adjudicator can charge for the time spent administering corrections (or even investigating such matters). In principle, we see no reason why not as a matter of contract, but we have always taken the view that it would be inappropriate to charge for our time attending to corrections. The question of whether to charge will ultimately be a matter for the individual adjudicator.

CONDUCT/CONTACT WITH PARTIES/REPRESENTATIVES

Most people will recognize that the obligation to act impartially and in a procedurally fair manner regulates the way adjudicators conduct themselves during the course of an adjudication. However, in our view this obligation also extends beyond the adjudication itself. We therefore believe that an adjudicator should be conscious of their behaviour and conduct post Decision as well as during the process. This is not restricted to any interactions with the parties or those who may have been involved with the adjudication itself, although this will be paramount.

There is the possibility that, following a Decision being issued, the adjudicator may come into contact with individuals who have been involved with the adjudication. To a certain extent, this may be inevitable, especially if the adjudicator is experienced and/or part of a relatively small 'dispute resolution' community. In some instances, the adjudicator will be aware of the identity of everyone involved in an adjudication, but this is not always the case. For example, as we mentioned in chapter 9, it is not uncommon for parties to involve counsel or experts as part of their 'team' but not disclose the fact to the adjudicator. The adjudicator should therefore be alive to that possibility.

In our view, it is inappropriate for an adjudicator to engage in discussions or to express a view on an adjudication that they have been involved with, whether that is with those individuals who were directly involved with the adjudication or otherwise. Even if the process is not expressed as confidential in the underlying legislation, rules, etc., it is generally considered to be confidential and the adjudicator should be mindful of this. However, the need for confidentiality is subject to one possible caveat: namely, that it may be possible to refer to a case without disclosing the parties' names or enabling those listening (or reading) to identify who the parties were or which adjudication is being referred to. It may not be particularly difficult to disguise the details in this way, but whether a case is referred to will depend on the approach of the individual adjudicator. If the adjudicator is at the guarded end of the spectrum of cautiousness, it may be that the best course of action for them to adopt is not to refer at all to situations they have experienced. However, some adjudicators may feel comfortable referring to their experiences, and, provided the parties' identities and the dispute/project are not disclosed, we see nothing intrinsically wrong with this. Indeed, shared experiences may assist with education and the development of best practice.

Another consideration for an adjudicator post Decision is their interactions (in a more general sense) with those individuals who have been involved with their adjudications. For example, an adjudicator may meet a party representative at a conference, seminar or work-related social event. In our view, an adjudicator should be sensitive to the possibility that there may be someone present who was also involved with that adjudication representing the other side. If the adjudicator was seen engaging in social discourse with one party, this could create difficulties and potentially lead to an issue or an allegation of impropriety. Although such a possibility may be remote, we nevertheless think that adjudicators should be careful in the way they conduct themselves.

ARCHIVING/SHREDDING/CONFIDENTIALITY

The adjudication process will have generated correspondence and documents, certainly electronically and very possibly in hard copy too. The question then arises of what the adjudicator should do with the correspondence and documents once the adjudication has finished. This question can be addressed in two ways: in the context of what may be required as a matter of law and in the context of practicality.

As a matter of law, there may be an obligation to maintain confidentiality in respect of documents that are retained by the adjudicator. There may also be an obligation to protect data included within documents that may have been provided in evidence in compliance with any data protection laws, e.g. personal information such as home addresses, bank account information or earnings. The adjudicator will need to take into account any obligations in these respects.

If we think of the reasons why an adjudicator may need to retain documentation provided in an adjudication, these are likely either to relate to a claim for unpaid fees or to address a complaint. Although the adjudicator will have knowledge of whether fees have been paid, they may not be aware of any complaint for some time after a Decision is published. We address how to deal with complaints and getting paid later in this chapter, but for present purposes the key consideration is a practical one regarding the extent to which it is necessary to keep documents in order to address any complaint or to support a claim for payment. If the documents are held electronically, retaining hard copies may not be necessary. If they are not, it will be a question of judgement as to whether retention of documents is necessary. The practice we tend to adopt is to retain any hard copies of documents that we have printed until we have been paid. We also include a provision in our terms that provides that documents will be destroyed within a prescribed period of time (or following payment if later) unless the parties advise us otherwise, e.g. if there are further adjudications between the parties, they may wish the adjudicator to retain documentation for that purpose.

As business increasingly moves towards only using electronic communications, the concept of disposal of paper documents may become less relevant. Nevertheless, even if submissions are exclusively electronic, the adjudicator may still elect to print some or all of what they receive. In light of any obligations in respect of confidentiality and data protection, it is important that documents are disposed of appropriately. Documents will therefore need to be destroyed so that their content is not disclosed, and we suggest that they are shredded in a commercially sensitive manner. We tend to use firms that specialize in providing such services, who will collect and then shred or destroy documents (including any data held on memory devices/sticks).

Retention and disposal of electronic documents will also need to be considered. In light of the points we have already made regarding confidentiality and data protection, we recommend that document security measures that restrict access are put in place to avoid any inadvertent disclosure. Additionally, there is the practical issue of data storage capacity, as the documents provided can have significant file sizes. We therefore recommend that electronic documents are removed/deleted either systematically or periodically in order to reduce the amount of data storage required. Nevertheless, we do retain an electronic copy of our Decisions and will also have copies of electronic communications stored in an electronic archive.

COMPLAINTS

The likelihood is that at least one of the parties will be unhappy with the outcome of the adjudication, and on occasion they may also be dissatisfied with the way the adjudication was conducted. This might result in a complaint by one of the parties, either to the organization who appointed the adjudicator or to one of the adjudicator's professional bodies. The adjudicator may consequently be required to respond to a complaint and/or they might be the subject of an investigation into the complaint.

Although a complaint may be unfounded or represent a case of sour grapes on the part of a losing party (or it might come from an 'embarrassed' party representative seeking to justify their actions and/or their fees), this does not obviate the need for an adjudicator to address the complaint. An adjudicator should therefore be prepared to justify their actions and their conduct, and they should keep this in mind throughout the process. To be clear, however, we consider accountability to be a positive thing as it guards against poor practice and complacency. It also ensures that users of adjudication maintain trust in the process, and we certainly do not believe that adjudicators are beyond reproach. Nor do we think that they should 'mark their own work' or be regulated solely by their peers.

When an adjudicator is faced with a complaint, we recommend they adopt a neutral or detached approach and try not to take the complaint personally. We recognize that this may be challenging, and we have personally experienced attacks where our integrity has been called into question. Nevertheless, our view is that (at least publicly) a measured, objective response is better than an overly emotional one, which may give the impression that the adjudicator is 'entering the arena'. As we have already said, a thick skin is an essential trait for an adjudicator. The bottom line is that complaints are likely to be made on occasion, and we encourage adjudicators to accept this possibility and recognize that it goes with the role and should not be taken too personally.

JUDICIAL COMMENT/ENFORCEABILITY

Although it is unlikely that the adjudicator will be involved in any enforcement proceedings or further proceedings regarding the underlying dispute, it is not unheard of. We know of examples where an adjudicator has either been asked to provide (or has voluntarily provided) evidence to a court in proceedings connected to an adjudication. However, this is not the norm, and we are also aware that some adjudicators will include a provision in their terms that they should not be called as a witness in any proceedings concerning the adjudication brought by the parties. In most cases, therefore, the adjudicator will not be party to any proceedings connected with the Decision.

Regardless of the jurisdiction, judgments regarding either the enforcement of an adjudicator's Decision or the underlying subject matter are regularly published. An example of the latter is where a party is seeking to reverse a decision in a hearing on a discrete point before a higher tribunal in order to 'trump' the adjudicator's Decision. In such circumstances, the identity of the adjudicator may become known, and it is also possible that the adjudicator will be subject to judicial comment, adverse or otherwise.

The adjudicator's need for a thick skin is never more relevant than when a judge includes criticism of an adjudicator's conduct or their conclusion on a substantive point. It is there for all the world to see, and it might even become the subject of legal articles or blogs. As many a first instance judge will tell you (perhaps tongue-in-cheek) when they have been overturned by an appeal court: 'Everyone is entitled to get it "wrong"!' The key is to try not to take criticism to heart. Conversely, we also believe an adjudicator should avoid getting carried away if a judge is complimentary or reaches a conclusion that mirrors theirs.

Thinking about the attributes of an adjudicator that are considered desirable, most would agree that the ability to be level headed and calm under pressure is a positive. With that in mind, our view is that it is undesirable to engage in any public discussion or to comment publicly on any judicial criticism, no matter how tempting it might be to do so. What is important is to reflect on what has been said to see whether any improvement is needed and/or whether, with the benefit of hindsight, a different approach might have been appropriate. In that way, lessons can be learned – not only for the adjudicator's benefit, but also for the benefit of others involved in adjudication, including other adjudicators. We certainly advocate that aspiring and practising adjudicators should take a keen interest in cases concerning adjudicators' Decisions, and should use them as a learning tool. As the saying goes: 'It's more enjoyable learning from other people's mistakes than your own!'

GETTING PAID

It is not unknown for adjudicators to have difficulty trying to secure payment of their fees. This is perhaps understandable when we consider the context in which an adjudication takes place. First, there will be a dispute. This may have been caused by cash flow issues for one or both of the parties, and it might result in an inability to pay. Second, the dispute will result in an outcome (in the form of a Decision) that is imposed by an adjudicator. This could lead to a party (or parties) who are unhappy with the Decision, and this in turn might result in a reluctance to pay the adjudicator.

Irrespective of the legal position, the adjudicator will need to take account of the commercial considerations associated with pursuing payment of unpaid fees. To a certain extent, the legal and commercial aspects may be related. For example, the adjudicator may seek to include provisions in their terms that afford them protection if it proves necessary to pursue unpaid fees. In particular, we are aware that some adjudicators provide for the possibility of them charging for any time spent personally chasing fees. This could then provide some solace if the adjudicator has to draft correspondence or prepare claim documents or a witness statement in support of a claim, and so on.

RELEVANT CASE LAW

In the UK case of *Steve Ward Services (UK) Ltd v Davies & Davies Associates Ltd*[2] the adjudicator successfully pursued one of the parties to an adjudication for his outstanding fees of £4,290 plus VAT. The adjudicator represented himself in the High Court and in the Court of Appeal and was awarded his costs based on the time he had spent on the case. The adjudicator's terms included a provision that his hourly rate would apply to all time spent, including 'in relation to securing unpaid fees, expenses and disbursements due'.

From a legal perspective, the adjudicator's entitlement to be paid will be derived from the applicable legislation and/or the applicable terms. The entitlement to payment may be the result of an express agreement or it may be implied, e.g. there may be an entitlement to be paid a reasonable fee. The adjudicator will therefore need to understand the underlying basis or cause of any action for a claim for unpaid fees. The adjudicator will also need to consider any objections to payment raised by the parties.

From a commercial perspective, the adjudicator will need to consider the financial position of the parties. Specifically, do they have the means to pay and/or are they solvent? If one of the parties is subject to insolvency proceedings, there may be an embargo on any proceedings being commenced against them. If that party is insolvent, the adjudicator will be left with the option of pursuing the solvent party and – although that party may feel a sense of injustice in the event that they have been successful in the adjudication – the adjudicator is usually entitled to pursue this course of action due to the joint and several nature of liability for their fees. The parties would (or at least should) have been aware of the fact that they are jointly and severally liable for an adjudicator's fees from the outset, and they can therefore have no complaints in this

2 [2022] EWCA Civ 153.

regard. If both parties are insolvent, the adjudicator is likely to be an unsecured creditor, and there will therefore be little that can be done to proactively recover any unpaid fees unless they have the benefit of a guarantee or an undertaking (e.g. from an insolvency practitioner or party representative).

If solvency is not an issue, the adjudicator will need to consider whether it is worth pursuing payment at all and, if it is, how to do so. In this regard, the adjudicator will need to assess how much time and resource may be required to pursue payment, as well as the legal costs of doing so, and then weigh that against the amount being claimed. The reality is that time will be required, and at some point the time and cost involved in pursuing a debt may not be commercially viable.

If an adjudicator decides to pursue payment of unpaid fees, we would suggest that a structured incremental approach is adopted. The reason for non-payment may actually not be a consequence of an inability or reluctance to pay, but rather the result of an inadvertent oversight or logistical issue. In this case, a simple prompt might result in payment by return. For this reason we recommend that the first step should be a polite chase or enquiry to ask the parties to attend to payment or to clarify the position. If this does not result in payment, we suggest a more formal ultimatum, perhaps specifying a date by which payment should be made, failing which the adjudicator may pursue payment by a formal means.

Chasing payment may elicit an acknowledgement that payment is due but also a claim that payment is not possible immediately because of financial circumstances. The party's response might also be accompanied by a proposal to pay the outstanding fees by instalments. Adjudicators are not obliged to agree to such terms but might consider it pragmatic to do so if the party in question has demonstrated that they cannot currently pay and the terms of payment can be agreed. For example, the adjudicator might insist on the party agreeing that, in the event that they default and fail to make a payment of an instalment, immediate payment of all outstanding sums would become due, plus interest.

If chasing does not result in payment or a proposed payment plan, the next step might be to commence court proceedings and issue a claim. The adjudicator could start the proceedings themselves or they could choose to engage external lawyers to manage the process. Again, this might require an element of assessing the commerciality of whether the amount claimed and the chances of success justify the expense of litigation.

As a final note, we would note that in the relatively low number of instances where we have had to pursue recovery of our fees through the courts, we have invariably obtained a judgment in our favour. Where the party has not had the means to pay, however, any 'victory' has to a certain extent been a hollow one. Nevertheless, a judgment might have other benefits, not least in respect of any complaint that may have been made.

CHAPTER 11

Three-person adjudications

Where adjudications are conducted under an adjudication scheme that has been mandated or imposed, it is more likely than not that the process will be conducted before a sole adjudicator. However, where adjudications are purely contractual, this is not always the case, especially where parties from different jurisdictions are involved, i.e. those that arise under or in connection with international contracts. For example, the FIDIC forms of contract that have dispute adjudication (and avoidance) boards (referred to as DABs or DAABs), and other projects that involve dispute review boards (DRBs), may provide for disputes to be referred to a DAB, DAAB or DRB, which can be constituted of one, three or more persons (usually an odd number). While such boards can also play a role in dispute avoidance, and they will sometimes attend site and project meetings, this chapter focuses on their adjudicative functions.

Where the adjudication is before a three-person tribunal, this will create a different dynamic from an adjudication before a sole adjudicator. At the very least it will throw up practical issues that need to be considered. The parties, for example, will need to account for the possibility that not all members of the adjudication panel will agree. For this reason, well-drafted procedures will provide that a majority Decision will be effective and/or that the 'chair' or the 'presiding adjudicator' will have supremacy in the event the adjudicators do not agree. This reflects the convention in international arbitration.

As well as considering the questions of conflicts of interest and availability (which will not differ from the situation where the tribunal is a sole adjudicator), each tribunal member will need to consider their terms and their fee arrangement. This may be the subject of discussion between the tribunal or it can be left to each tribunal member to agree and/or set. In our experience, each tribunal member's terms fall to be considered separately, and separate contractual relationships between the parties and each individual tribunal member should be created.

On a practical level, members of a three-person adjudication panel will also need to agree between themselves about how they will deal with procedural and case management issues and, ultimately, about how they will reach and produce their Decision. It is therefore important to agree and set some ground rules in that respect.

In our view, there is much to learn from the field of international arbitration, where three-person tribunals are prevalent. We therefore advocate that the tribunal (led by its chair) liaises at an early stage in order to agree how procedural issues should be addressed. In our experience, it is typical for the chair to lead the procedural correspondence, but we consider it good practice for the chair to have sought and obtained agreement from their co-adjudicators as to how they should address procedural issues. For example, it might be agreed that simple acknowledgements or agreement of parties' agreed amendments to timetable, etc., may be addressed by the chair without obtaining specific agreement from the co-adjudicators, but that more complex issues may require consultation and agreement as to the appropriate response and approach to adopt. For those more experienced with acting as sole adjudicator this may feel a bit odd and burdensome, but the upside is that the collective minds may provide some comfort, especially in situations that might not have been experienced before.

As well as addressing procedural and case management matters, the tribunal may be involved with meetings with the parties, either online or in person. There might also be a site inspection. In such situations, the tribunal will need to consider in advance how such meetings or site inspections will be managed. For example, who is going to lead any questioning or interaction with the parties? Where the tribunal is multidisciplinary or has divergent levels or areas of expertise, this might lend itself to any questioning being distributed between the tribunal to suit their expertise or experience.

In an online situation, the tribunal will need to consider how its members can interact or converse during the meeting. If convenient, the tribunal might agree to be in one 'room' so that they can either converse or pass messages between themselves in the same way they would if convening the meeting in person. Alternatively, a separate group chat could be set up for this purpose.

The other aspect of meetings and site inspections that will need to be considered is the additional difficulty of coordinating three diaries. Although this is not always an issue, it can lead to delays that might otherwise not have been encountered if a sole adjudicator had been appointed.

The main area in which the dynamic of having a three-person tribunal rather than a single adjudicator can make the overall timetable longer is the process of reaching and producing the Decision. Whereas case management should not create too much of an additional burden compared with adjudications before a sole adjudicator, it will be rare for a Decision before a three-person tribunal to have been reached without some form of deliberation, drafting, redrafting and reworking. This will inevitably add time to the process.

There is no prescribed approach to how a Decision may be reached, drafted and published by a three-person adjudication tribunal, but again, the world of international arbitration may be a source of guidance here. The first step is to reach agreement on which issues (including any applicable sub-issues) fall to be determined. To a certain extent this may have already been established, especially if there has been a meeting with the parties and/or if the tribunal has had the opportunity to discuss and agree prior to the close of submissions.

Once the issues have been agreed, the next step will be for the members of the tribunal to reach their conclusion on each issue. This may be something that lends itself to immediate discussion, or it might require some further analysis or investigation. If the latter, then time will be needed for this purpose, and arrangements will need to be made for the conclusions to be shared and/or discussed between the tribunal members. It may also be sensible for the tribunal to attempt to reach a conclusion on any preliminary or preceding issues, such as liability, before considering subsequent issues such as quantum, especially if there has been an agreement to delegate any aspects of the decision-making process or analysis to a particular tribunal member. For example, if one of the tribunal members is a delay analyst or a quantity surveyor, it may be desirable – and more cost effective – for them to undertake any initial analysis of the evidence provided in respect of delay or quantum issues, respectively.

The mechanics of how the deliberations work may differ, but the important thing is that each member has the opportunity to provide their view or conclusion on each issue. This may be in the form of an email exchange or a further meeting, either online or in person. Where there is agreement between all three adjudicators, it will simply be a matter of recording such agreement, but where there is disagreement, the chair will need to navigate discussions such that any disagreement does not adversely affect the progress of further deliberations and/or the production of the Decision. In practice, where there is disagreement there may be an element of negotiation between the tribunal members. The personality of the individual who disagrees with the majority may also have an effect. For some it may be easy to put disagreement on a preliminary/liability issue to one side and to engage in deliberations on subsequent issues. Others, though, might not find themselves able to do so. Although this can create difficulties, the safety valve of having an odd number of tribunal members should ensure that a Decision is nevertheless reached and published.

Once the tribunal has reached its conclusion or decision on each issue, either unanimously or by majority, the Decision will need to be drafted. Again, sometimes the nature of the dispute referred and the composition of the panel mean that delegation of parts of the drafting to individual tribunal members is possible. However, where this is done, we consider it important that one member (typically the chair) takes responsibility for incorporating separate sections together into one document and ensuring that the document is internally consistent.

Prior to drafting commencing on the substantive issues, we consider it sensible for the tribunal to discuss and agree the reasons for their conclusions on each issue. Thereafter, it is a matter of those tasked with drafting to provide a draft for consideration by the other tribunal members. Again, time will need to be made and diarized for this task in order to avoid any unnecessary delay. The use of tracked changes and comments can be helpful in this regard, although this will still need managing in terms of the sequence in which any suggested edits or comments are incorporated and administered.

We have already alluded to the possibility that a Decision may be reached by agreement between all three tribunal members or by a majority. Where there is disagreement on an issue and/or the overall conclusion, thought will need to be given as to how that is dealt with in the context of the Decision. It may be that the minority tribunal member is content for no reference to be made to the fact that a Decision was reached by a majority. Where this is not the case, the chair will need to consider an appropriate form of words to record the fact that the tribunal were not in total agreement on an issue. However, the question then arises as to whether there is any utility in such a record being made, and it also needs to be decided whether the reasons for any disagreement are included in the Decision. On the one hand, the 'dissent' has no value: it will not affect the temporarily binding nature of the Decision and it could undermine the parties' confidence in the Decision. On the other hand, it may give the losing party some comfort to know that its case was arguable and found some accord with at least one of the tribunal members. The decision over whether to make any reference to, and/or give reasons for, a minority view will ultimately be something for the chair to make.

As when a Decision is produced by a sole adjudicator, we consider it prudent to have a fresh pair of eyes to undertake proofing of the Decision before it is published. Again, this will need to be coordinated and managed by the chair.

The final point to consider is the post-Decision matters, such as administration of any corrections and the collection of fees. To a certain extent, corrections can be dealt with in the same way as other case management procedural matters. So, typically, the chair will take the lead and consider whether any further deliberation is needed, and they will thereafter administer or delegate any corrections or response to any request for corrections. In relation to fee collection, in the event the tribunal did not have the benefit of a lien, this will typically ultimately fall to each individual tribunal member.

CHAPTER 12

Concluding thoughts

When we started out as adjudicators, there was little by way of guidance as to how to conduct an adjudication or reach a Decision. To a certain extent this was understandable: the process was new and there was uncertainty as to how adjudication would work in practice. The question of how supervising courts would treat adjudicators' Decisions, and what effect Decisions would have, was unanswered. The process has developed over time, and although there is more clarity now, there is a greater degree of complexity than was perhaps initially anticipated. It is also probably fair to say that the use of adjudication is greater than could reasonably have been envisaged. Consequently, we consider that there is a greater need for guidance for those who act, or who aspire to act, as adjudicators.

We hope that this book provides a practical guide to those who either act or aspire to act as adjudicators of construction and engineering disputes. It draws primarily on our collective experience, and we hope that it will help those charged with the conduct of adjudications to navigate the process.

We have aimed to provide a 'cradle to grave' walkthrough, starting with the appointment, then timetabling and procedural issues, how to deal with any jurisdictional issues, submissions and evidence, whether to convene meetings and site inspections (and if so, how), how to formulate the issues that may fall to be decided, how to reach and draft the Decision, and finally how to manage post-Decision issues such as administration of any corrections. Along the way we have sought to share some observations regarding the types of disputes and parties that might be encountered, and we have also given our thoughts regarding the distinguishing features of three-person adjudication tribunals.

In our view, one of the great attributes of adjudication is the flexibility it affords both the adjudicator and the parties to adopt a procedure that suits the particular dispute that has been referred to adjudication. There is therefore no 'one size fits all' approach, and we are conscious that the way we elect to conduct an adjudication may differ from the approach of other practitioners. Indeed, the approach that each of us adopts can sometimes differ. Nevertheless, we believe that there are some key fundamental principles that will apply irrespective of the applicable governing legislation or the procedural rules. We would therefore encourage adjudicators to develop their own individual style and approach.

We have both derived an enormous amount of personal and professional satisfaction from acting as adjudicators, and we realize how fortunate we are to have been afforded the opportunity to fulfil this role. We have learned so much along the way, and we continue to learn, and we hope that by sharing some of our knowledge in this book we will assist a future generation of adjudicators to provide a much-needed service for the benefit of those who find themselves in construction and engineering disputes.

APPENDIX A

How to become an adjudicator?

The focus of this book has been on the practice of adjudication from the perspective of an adjudicator or an adjudication tribunal. However, one thing we have not addressed is the question of how someone becomes an adjudicator in the first place. This appendix therefore seeks to cover the steps that someone might follow if they wish to practise as an adjudicator.

Although there are typically no restrictions on who can be an adjudicator, and the parties to a dispute are generally free to agree the identity of their adjudicator, the reality is that it is unlikely for parties to agree to appoint someone unless they already have a track record or experience of acting as an adjudicator. As such, the more conventional way of someone being appointed as an adjudicator for the first time will be as a result of a nomination by an ANA/ANB.

Most ANAs/ANBs will set down certain criteria that will need to be satisfied if someone wishes to be included on their list or roster. Typically, this will be a combination of professional qualifications, specific adjudication training and experience. Additionally, there might be a requirement to undertake some form of assessment of a person's ability to manage the adjudication process and produce a reasoned Decision. It is therefore sensible for anyone who wishes to become an adjudicator to research and establish what specific criteria each ANA or ANB requires in order to identify whether any further study or experience is required.

ADJUDICATORS' BACKGROUNDS

Adjudicators will typically be expected to have experience of the construction or engineering industries, either as a construction or engineering professional or as a lawyer who has been involved with construction projects or disputes in an advisory capacity. In our experience, it is unusual for an adjudicator to have no professional qualification. The expectation is therefore likely to be that an adjudicator is either a qualified construction industry professional or a lawyer with experience of construction law, and in practice many adjudicators are dual qualified.

The background of construction professionals can be varied. We typically encounter quantity surveyors, civil engineers and architects, but we also sometimes see more specialist professions, such as building surveyors and building services engineers. The legal profession is also well represented among adjudicators, and the commonality is that the adjudicator will almost invariably have a primary professional qualification. In turn, in order to qualify in a primary profession, individuals will typically have had to have undertaken a combination of academic training and practical or vocational experience in order to qualify in the first place. This will take time.

As well as having a relevant primary profession, some ANAs and ANBs will also prescribe a set number of years of post-qualification experience, and in our experience ten years is common. This probably reflects the expectation from users of adjudication that an adjudicator will have sufficient experience of construction projects and/or disputes to be familiar with the type of project or dispute that is the subject of any adjudication before them.

A consequence of the professional and post-qualification criteria is that an adjudicator is unlikely to be in their 20s. If we think of the length of time it takes to qualify as a construction professional or lawyer, most professionals will likely be in their mid 20s before qualifying. If we add to that a ten-year post-qualification requirement, it is easy to understand why we do not see many adjudicators under the age of 30.

Although there are no restrictions in terms of gender, the majority of adjudicators thus far are male. A report published by King's College London in collaboration with the Adjudication Society in 2022 found that less than 8% of adjudicators in the United Kingdom were female.[1] We suspect that this pattern is repeated in other jurisdictions. To a certain

1 Centre of Construction Law & Dispute Resolution, King's College London. 2022. 2022 construction adjudication in the United Kingdom: tracing trends and guiding reform. Report, October.

certain extent it probably reflects the fact that, at least initially, the pool of adjudicators was drawn from experienced construction industry professionals who were themselves predominantly male. The current gender split in the United Kingdom when it comes to newly qualified construction industry professionals (approximately 20% female) and lawyers (approximately 50%) indicates that there is an under-representation of female adjudicators, but we hope that in time, the gender split shifts in line with the increasing number of female construction professionals, as well as a tendency towards legally qualified adjudicators. All that said, we believe that positive action is required to improve the profile and representation of women as adjudicators, and we are aware that, in light of the previously mentioned report from the Adjudication Society and King's College, there are a number of initiatives being implemented that are aimed at increasing the number of female adjudicators.[2]

TRAINING/ACADEMIC REQUIREMENTS

When adjudication commenced in the United Kingdom there was a need for ANBs to be set up and then a need for those bodies to establish lists of adjudicators. Although some new bodies were created, in the main, it was professional organizations that held themselves out as nominating bodies. Perhaps understandably, these bodies looked towards construction industry arbitrators who were either already on a roster of arbitrators and/or who had experience of conducting arbitrations and producing awards. However, these organizations also recognized that some additional training was required in order to prepare these individuals for what was then a new form of dispute resolution.

In light of the fact that the path to becoming an arbitrator in the construction industry had involved an initial primary profession, a prescribed period of post-qualification experience, an arbitration qualification (involving examination in law, evidence, case management, award writing) and a pupillage, the belief was that a relatively short training adjudication course

2 For example, the UK Adjudication Society has established a Women in Adjudication Group, which is tasked with the promotion of women in adjudication, with training and with collecting qualitative data to understand why women's participation is currently so low. The society has also created the Equal Representation in Adjudication Pledge, which is a commitment to improving the profile and representation of women as adjudicators in the United Kingdom.

lasting, say, one day or perhaps a weekend was adequate. Additionally, for those who were perhaps less experienced, or who had not practised as an arbitrator, there may have been a requirement to prepare a Decision based on a hypothetical scenario and/or to attend an interview.

As the uptake of adjudication increased in the United Kingdom, so did the level of complexity of the disputes being referred to adjudication. However, the increase in the use and popularity of adjudication corresponded with a reduction in the use of construction arbitration for determining domestic (i.e. non-international) construction disputes. As a consequence, as well as an increase in the demand for suitably qualified adjudicators, there was a diminishing pool of individuals who had undertaken training in and/or had experience of case management, deciding or determining a dispute, and preparing an award or Decision. As a response to this, organizations such as the Chartered Institute of Arbitrators and the RICS (who both had experience of delivering training courses in arbitration) undertook to deliver more extensive training courses that were solely focused on adjudication. These typically took the form of post-graduate diplomas.

The content of these courses was and is very much modelled on the post-graduate diploma courses that are in place for arbitration. Therefore, after a preliminary introduction to adjudication, there will be a requirement to study and take exams in the law of obligations (with an emphasis on contract) and the law of evidence for those who have not already studied these topics (e.g. those who are not qualified lawyers). Additionally, there will be a requirement to study and be tested on the applicable legislation, procedural rules and jurisprudence relating to adjudication in the relevant jurisdiction. There will also be a requirement to undertake training and assessment in respect of case management and reaching and producing a Decision. Typically, these courses will be delivered on a part-time basis over a period of twelve to eighteen months.

As well as courses dedicated to adjudication, there has also been an increase in the prevalence of modules on the law of adjudication and Decision writing in post-graduate programmes such as MSc degrees and LLMs in construction law and dispute resolution. This reflects both the prominence and the importance of adjudication in the field of dispute resolution in the UK construction industry – and, increasingly, further afield as well.

So now, as well as possessing a primary profession and having (say) ten years of post-qualification relevant industry work experience, prospective adjudicators are typically required to have undertaken and/or possess a post-graduate qualification in adjudication.

THE ATTRIBUTES OF AN ADJUDICATOR

Having the ability and the means to obtain the prerequisite qualifications is one part of the journey towards becoming an adjudicator. Another part is having the aptitude for undertaking the role. Knowledge of the law, construction technology, construction contracts, procedural rules and an encyclopaedic knowledge of both the jurisprudence surrounding adjudication and the latest developments in case law does not mean that someone is necessarily well suited to and/or will enjoy the role of adjudicating. That said, it might help!

If we think about the functions an adjudicator performs and the environment in which they operate, one of the key characteristics is that the role is typically a solitary one. Even where an adjudication tribunal consists of three members, each adjudicator has to work independently and exercise his or her own personal judgement. There might also be either an express or an implied obligation of confidentiality. Additionally, an adjudicator might have to keep their distance from parties and their representatives at events or even decline invitations to attend events in order to avoid any suggestions of perceived bias. It is therefore sometimes said that the role of an adjudicator can be a lonely one. Although there may be an opportunity to meet and discuss issues and experiences on a confidential basis with fellow adjudicators, it is fair to say that if you are someone who prefers working as part of a team or on a collaborative basis, the role of adjudicator may not be for you. The ability to work independently and on your own will therefore be a desirable attribute.

As well as the ability to work alone, adjudicators need to have good time management skills. Key characteristics of adjudication are the tight time constraints that are imposed and the fast-track nature of the process. The adjudicator will therefore need to be able to manage their own diary and ensure that there is sufficient time available to attend to ongoing case management matters; to review the submissions; to conduct their investigation or interrogation of the evidence; and to reach, draft and publish their Decision. This will require discipline. It will also require the ability to work under the pressure of a time deadline.

Another aspect of the job is to identify and formulate the issues to be decided and to undertake an analysis of the legal submissions and the evidence, which could be factual, technical or opinion. This will require good analytical skills, and, again, the ability to undertake the necesary work under the pressure of a time deadline is an essential skill. Allied to this attribute is the ability to exercise judgement in a measured way.

Although it sounds obvious, an adjudicator will need to possess the ability to make a decision. There is no room for indecisiveness or for 'sitting on the fence'. While, admittedly, an adjudicator always has the option of 'not being persuaded', this does not obviate the need for a decision to be made. The reality is that not all individuals have the ability to reach a decision independently and without the opportunity to consult someone or 'phone a friend'. A decisive character is therefore a necessary attribute, but decisiveness should of course always be subject to decisions being made after an appropriate degree of analysis and the exercise of judgement. Irrespective of the outcome, the parties will require a clear decision so that they know what has been decided and can implement the Decision without any uncertainty.

CAREER PATH: GETTING YOUR FIRST APPOINTMENT

In our experience, the number of individuals who would fall into the category of 'career adjudicators', i.e. those who exclusively act as adjudicators, is relatively small. However, the number of individuals who specialize in dispute resolution more generally, and perhaps perform different roles in conjunction with practising as an adjudicator, is larger. Some of these roles may be similar in that they represent a third-party neutral function, e.g. acting as an arbitrator, a dispute board member, an expert determiner or a mediator. Others may be less similar, e.g. providing advice, representing parties by preparing and/or defending claims, acting as an expert witness, etc. There are also a significant number of adjudicators who spend the majority of their time on live projects or in their primary professional role.

And even among the few career adjudicators, it is very unlikely that they fell into that category from their first appointment. This reflects the reality that parties are unlikely to agree to the appointment of an adjudicator without a track record, and it is also testament to the fact that ANAs and ANBs are likely to limit and/or monitor early appointments in order to assess an adjudicator's ability. Although some ANAs/ANBs operate 'cab rank' appointment policies, others will look to appoint the 'right horse' for the 'right course', and it is perhaps understandable that they are more likely to turn to known entities for more complex matters.

In light of the foregoing, it is probably unwise to be too prescriptive about how to develop a career as an adjudicator, save to say that, if you are fortunate enough to receive an appointment, attempt to do a good job in a conscientious manner! The path to obtaining a first appointment is also likely to vary, but in our view the first objective should be to be admitted onto a list or roster of adjudicators, as that is where an adjudicator is most likely to receive their first appointment.

As well as setting academic and professional qualification requirements, some ANAs and ANBs will also require some form of application or assessment process. Applicants will typically be required to detail their dispute resolution experience, and we would therefore recommend that those aspiring to act as adjudicators seek to gain such experience. If this is possible within an individual's employment, that may be less problematic than if an individual's employment situation does not expose them to any formal dispute resolution proceedings. In these circumstances, it may be necessary either to seek alternative employment where there are such opportunities or to seek permission or support to secure experience. For example, it may be possible to seek a placement or secondment or to obtain a pupillage or a shadowing opportunity. Some ANAs and ANBs recognize shadowing or pupillage as part of their experience requirements.

It is likely that another aspect of the application process will be demonstrating a current awareness of the latest developments in adjudication and complying with any continuing professional development (CPD) obligations. In our view, CPD needs to be specific and relevant to adjudication. We would therefore recommend that aspiring adjudicators seek membership of organizations such as the Society of Construction Law and the Chartered Institute of Arbitrators, both of which organize events on dispute resolution throughout the world, and also country-specific organizations such as the Adjudication Society in the United Kingdom. We would also encourage active involvement in these organizations, e.g. getting involved in committees or working groups. As well as providing valuable CPD and awareness of the latest relevant developments, it will provide the opportunity to network. It may also offer an opportunity to meet and converse with practising adjudicators, which may be useful for obtaining pupillage as well as being a potential source of references from experienced practitioners in support of any application to be included on an ANB or ANA list or roster.

The key take-home message from us is that aspiring adjudicators need to get involved in the field of dispute resolution and commit to keeping up to date with the latest developments. There is no reason why this should not commence in advance of or in conjunction with undertaking training or studying in adjudication, but it is even more important that this involvement happens after training and/or study as a stepping stone towards obtaining that elusive first appointment.

PUPILLAGE

Although we are unaware of any formal requirements for those applying to be included on lists or rosters of adjudicators to have undertaken pupillage, our view is that instigating such a requirement would be a sensible development. It is notable that, in response to complaints from aspiring adjudicators that ANAs and ANBs were requiring applicants to have acted as an adjudicator and/or produced a Decision, some practitioners now offer pupillage opportunities in an attempt to address the 'chicken and egg' conundrum.

As the realm of adjudication has no formal pupillage process – such as that operated by the Bar Council of England & Wales for those who wish to practise as barristers, for example – the precise mechanics of how a pupillage might work is likely to differ. That said, we are able to speak about our own experience of conducting pupillages.

Those who seek a pupillage with us must have already fulfilled the academic requirements to enable them to be admitted to a list or roster of adjudicators, although they need not have actually conducted an adjudication as an adjudicator. The rationale for this is that the purpose of the pupillage is to give pupils the opportunity to conduct an adjudication, not to 'teach' them how to adjudicate. That said, we appreciate that, in practice, a pupil is likely to learn through a combination of doing (in a safe environment) and observing how someone else conducts an adjudication (ideally in a 'live' environment).

The parties to a live adjudication will obviously need to consent to a pupil being involved. To this end, we would expect the adjudicator either to include a provision in their terms that they can involve a pupil or to seek confirmation from the parties that they have no objections to a pupil being involved. We also recommend that the adjudicator secures an undertaking that the pupil treats all matters as confidential, and that this undertaking is relayed to the parties. Additionally, we recommend that the adjudicator makes it clear that the pupil will not be involved in any substantive or procedural decisions (that being left to the adjudicator) and that there will be no charge to the parties. A copy of the proposed pupil's CV will typically be provided to the parties.

Prior to disclosing a proposed pupil's CV, we would suggest that the proposed pupil is asked to confirm whether there is any conflict with the parties. To do this, the adjudicator will have to share the names of the parties (and potentially the representatives and details of the project) on a confidential basis. Obtaining confirmation that there is no conflict means that the adjudicator potentially avoids wasting time in sharing details of a pupil who may not be accepted by the parties on account of a known conflict.

Again in the interests of avoiding wasting time, we would recommend not sharing details of the pupil and/or seeking specific consent until after it is known that the adjudication is proceeding. Typically, therefore, we share details only after the Referral is served. Once consent or confirmation of no objection is obtained, the process of shadowing can begin.

Our aim at the outset of the pupil's involvement is to get them up to speed as soon as possible so that they are dealing with matters in real time. In order to achieve this there will be an element of 'catching up' to do. In the modern era of electronic communications, the sharing of documents and correspondence is relatively straightforward – a considerable improvement on the situation that previously existed, where arbitration pupillages involved documents being copied, printed and/or posted or pupils having to attend their pupil supervisor's office to inspect said documents.

The approach we adopt is to send the initial enquiry to the pupil and ask them to send us their response as if they were responding to the

ANA/ANB or to the party representative(s). Once the pupil's response is received, we share with them our response (for comparison) and then send them confirmation of the nomination or agreement of the parties and ask them to draft their first communication to the parties, again sending it to us (as if to the parties). This will require the pupil to have thought about and prepared terms of appointment and initial directions. Once that is done, we share our communication and provide access to the Referral, typically via a download link. We also ask them to draft their next communication to the parties, which may include directions regarding the timetable and the procedure to be adopted.

Thereafter, we ask the pupil to address any challenges to jurisdiction or timetabling issues. In the same way, we ask the pupil to draft their communications and have a go themselves before we share how we actually dealt with any procedural issues. We tend not to converse with the pupil extensively during the course of the adjudication. This is in line with the intention to give the pupil the opportunity to conduct the adjudication as if they were the adjudicator and to make it as realistic as possible. However, we accept that the pupil will be constrained by the timetable, the procedure and the approach adopted by the actual adjudicator.

Hopefully, by the time the Response is served, the pupil will be in real time, such that communications can be shared almost instantaneously. If there is a meeting or a site inspection, we invite the pupil to attend if possible. If the pupil attends, we brief them to come along as an observer and we direct them not to intervene or interfere with the conduct of the meeting or inspection. Again, the approach we adopt is not to converse extensively regarding the evidence or submissions during the adjudication itself.

Once submissions have closed, the pupil will be asked to produce a Decision. In order to make the shadowing as realistic as possible we encourage pupils to attempt to complete their Decision by the actual Decision date, or as soon after it as possible. However, we also make it clear that we do not wish to see the pupil's Decision until after the time for correction of any slips or errors has expired. This is to avoid any suggestion that we may have been influenced by the pupil's Decision in the event there was an issue regarding a correction.

Finally, once Decisions have been exchanged, we ask the pupil to review and compare Decisions before setting up a debrief during which we will discuss the Decision and the overall process. This is where we would endeavour to discuss any particular issues that arose and make recommendations for improvements, as well as answering any questions the pupil might have. We then move on to the next shadowing opportunity until the pupil has completed and produced three Decisions, after which we provide a letter recording this fact, which the pupil may use in support of any applications to be admitted to a list or roster of adjudicators. We ask pupils to ensure that, if they are asked to provide copies of any of their Decisions (or directions/correspondence), they suitably anonymize them (thus preserving confidentiality) and also make clear that they were acting as a pupil and not the actual adjudicator.

Although we understand that pupils may be juggling their pupillage with a day job or other personal or family commitments, we encourage them to try and attend to procedural correspondence and to produce their Decisions in a timely manner. We have already alluded to the fact that this will make the experience more realistic, and it will also reduce the burden on the adjudicator, who has given their time freely: if the adjudicator has to trawl back through emails in order to feed through correspondence, or re-acquaint themself with a Decision issued some months previously, this is not ideal.

MENTORING

Mentoring refers here to situations in which a practising adjudicator is allocated with a mentor. This may be because of a policy of an ANB or ANA in respect of new adjudicators, or it could be on account of concerns that have been raised. The underlying purpose is to assist the adjudicator by giving them the ability to confer with their mentor (a more experienced adjudicator) if they required any assistance.

Although we very much support the concept of mentoring, we believe certain safeguards need to be put in place to ensure that the adjudicator who is being mentored (the 'mentee') does not breach any confidentiality obligations and also to ensure that the adjudicator does not delegate their function as adjudicator. In our view, the issue of confidentiality can be addressed by the adjudicator who is being mentored incorporating a provision in their terms to the effect that all matters will be treated as confidential, save as to comply with any obligations owed to an ANB, an ANA or a professional body.

When we have acted as mentors, we have been careful to ensure that we do not interfere with the adjudicator's decision making, either in relation to procedural and jurisdictional issues or in relation to the Decision itself. The aim is to provide guidance or assistance where needed, and rather than being instructive mentoring typically involves responding to queries with answers such as: 'Have you thought of this approach?" Again, we believe that a mentor should not impose their methods on the adjudicator, but should instead be there as a helping hand if needed, i.e. mentors should apply a light-touch approach in which they share the benefit of their experiences with the less experienced adjudicator as they develop.

CPD

We have already mentioned CPD in the context of the requirements of ANAs and ANBs for applicants. However, it is also extremely likely that, once an adjudicator is added to a list or roster, they will have an ongoing obligation to undertake CPD. We again believe that this should be adjudication specific. Without labouring the point, it is important for adjudicators to keep up to date on developments within the jurisdictions in which they are adjudicating. As well as joining organizations such as the Society of Construction Law, the Adjudication Society and the Chartered Institute of Arbitrators – and participating in their activities once signed up – we would strongly encourage practising adjudicators to attend conferences and keep abreast of relevant case law. We also recommend that adjudicators build time into their weekly (or daily) routines to review the latest published judgments that involve adjudicator's Decisions.

APPENDIX B

Example Decision

The example Decision given in the following pages is intended to illustrate how an adjudication Decision will be set out, albeit reformatted to suit the book. We must also emphasize that each adjudicator will develop their own individual style, and provided the essential elements are included there is not necessarily a right or wrong way to lay out a Decision.

The Decision itself concerns a relatively simple UK payment dispute and is based on a Decision that one of us wrote (it has been suitably anonymized to ensure confidentiality). We encourage readers to refer to it as they review the elements of chapter 9 concerning the structure of Decisions.

The appointment followed a nomination by an ANB/ANA, and there were no jurisdictional challenges. Had there been any such challenges, we would normally include a section titled 'Jurisdiction' after that titled 'The Issues' in which we would set out our conclusions on our jurisdiction.

Readers will note that we have set out the matters that are common ground between the parties, and have then gone on to summarize the parties' cases. We have then set out our findings, including reasons. The reasons are set out in list form, but there is no reason why they could not have been set out as a descriptive commentary. As we stress in chapter 9, what is important is that the reader (and especially the losing party) understands why the adjudicator has decided in the way they have. We certainly hope that readers are satisfied that we have passed the 'Why test" we describe in chapter 9!

IN THE MATTER OF AN ADJUDICATION BETWEEN:

BOTTOMLEY HACKETT CONSTRUCTION LIMITED

Referring Party

and

JONES GLENN DEVELOPMENTS LIMITED

Responding Party

ADJUDICATOR'S DECISION

Reached on 4 October 2023

By:

Mr Thomas Marks
MCMS Limited
45 Tabernacle Street
London
EC2A 4AA

CONTENTS

APPOINTMENT AND TIMETABLE

1. Following an application by Bottomley Hackett Construction Limited (BHC) to the Royal Institution of Chartered Surveyors dated 5 September 2023, I was appointed on 6 September 2023 to adjudicate a dispute arising under a contract between BHC and Jones Glenn Developments Limited (JGD). Under the contract, JGD engaged BHC to design and construct a fourteen-unit residential apartment block, including external works, at 202–262 Mouzer Road, London NW3 ('the Works'), for the sum of £5,298,769.00.[1]

2. The contract comprises an amended JCT Design and Build Contract, 2016 edition, and the documents appended thereto ('the Contract'). Article 7 and clause 9.2 of the Contract provide that any dispute or difference arising under the Contract may be referred to adjudication in accordance with the Scheme for Construction Contracts (England and Wales) Regulations 1998 (as amended) ('the Scheme'). This adjudication has therefore been conducted in accordance with the adjudication provisions in the Scheme.

1 All sums in this Decision are exclusive of VAT unless otherwise stated.

3. The dispute was referred to me on 7 September 2023, and I was therefore obliged to reach my Decision on or before 5 October 2023. I have complied with my obligation to reach my Decision by that date.

THE NATURE OF THE DISPUTE

4. The dispute concerns BHC's entitlement to payment for the sum claimed in its Interim Payment Application 13 (IPA13) dated 30 June 2023 (adjusted to take account of a subsequent payment) as a result of the alleged failure by JGD's employer's agent, Willet & Mohammed LLP (W&M), to serve a valid Pay Less Notice.

5. BHC contends that the sum claimed in IPA13 (as adjusted) should have been paid by the final date for payment and that JGD is in breach of the Contract by failing to pay this sum. BHC therefore claims that it is entitled to payment of the sum of £476,986.22, plus interest, in this adjudication. JGD submits that W&M served a valid Pay Less Notice and that, as such, BHC is not entitled to payment of the sum claimed.

SUBMISSIONS

6. In this adjudication BHC was represented by Beaumont Legal Services Limited and JGD was represented by Dysons LLP, who instructed Counsel, Mr Robert Kempe. I am grateful to the parties, their representatives and Counsel for their cooperation and assistance during this adjudication.

7. I have received the following written submissions from the parties in relation to the substantive issues.

   (i) BHC's Referral received on 7 September 2023 ('the Referral').

   (ii) JGD's Response received on 20 September 2023 ('the Response').

   (iii) BHC's Reply received on 26 September 2023 ('the Reply').

8. I confirm that I have read all of the parties' submissions and have taken them into account when reaching my Decision.

9. BHC has asked me to provide reasons for my Decision, and I have complied with its request.

REDRESS SOUGHT

10. The redress sought by BHC in the Referral is as follows:

> '27. BHC therefore asks the Adjudicator to decide as follows:
> (i) that JGD is in breach of contract as alleged and/or as the Adjudicator otherwise decides;
> (ii) that JGD pay BHC the sum of £476,986.22 or such other sum as the Adjudicator decides;
> (iii) that JGD pay BHC interest at £88.21 per day since 5 August;
> (iv) that JGD pay the Adjudicator's costs and expenses;
> (v) that all payments be made by JGD forthwith.'

THE ISSUES

11. In order to deal with the redress sought by BHC I need to address the following issues.

- Issue 1. Is BHC entitled to payment in this adjudication and, if so, how much?

- Issue 2. Is BHC entitled to interest and, if so, how much?

DECISION

ISSUE I. IS BHC ENTITLED TO PAYMENT IN THIS ADJUDICATION AND, IF SO, HOW MUCH?

12. The following clauses of the Contract are relevant to Issue 1.

> **'Interim Payments – Contractor's Interim Payment Applications, due dates and Payment Notices**
>
> . . .
>
> 4.7.3 In relation to each Interim Payment, the Contractor shall make an application to the Employer (an 'Interim Payment Application'), stating the sum that the Contractor considers to be due to him at the due date and the basis on which that sum has been calculated. Where the Interim Payment Application is received no later than the relevant Interim Valuation Date, the due date shall be the date that would apply under clause 4.7.2; if the Interim Payment Application is received later, the due date shall be 7 days after the date of receipt by the Employer.
>
> . . .
>
> 4.7.5 Not later than 5 days after each due date the Employer shall give a notice (a 'Payment Notice') to the Contractor, stating the sum that he considers to be or have been due to the Contractor at the due date, calculated in accordance with clause 4.12 or 4.13 and clause 4.14, and the basis on which that sum has been calculated.
>
> . . .
>
> **Interim and final payments – final date and amount**
>
> . . .
>
> 4.9.1 The final date for payment of each Interim Payment and the final payment shall be 28 days from its due date.
>
> . . .
>
> 4.9.3 If a Payment Notice is not given in accordance with clause 4.7.5, the Employer shall, subject to any Pay Less Notice under clause 4.9.5, pay the Contractor the sum stated as due in the Interim Payment Application.
>
> . . .
>
> 4.9.5 Where
>
> > 4.9.5.1 the Employer intends to pay less than the sum stated as due from him in a Payment Notice or Interim Payment Application; or
> >
> > . . .

> the Party by whom the payment is stated to be payable shall not later than 5 days before the final date for payment give the other Party notice of that intention in accordance with clause 4.10.1 (a 'Pay Less Notice').
>
> ...
>
> **Pay Less Notice and other general provisions**
>
> ...
>
> 4.10.1 A Pay Less Notice given by either Party shall specify the sum he considers to be due to the other Party at the date the notice is given and the basis on which that sum has been calculated.'

13. The following is common ground for the purposes of this adjudication.

    (i) IPA13 was submitted on the relevant Interim Valuation Date, 30 June 2023, and, as such, pursuant to clause 4.7.2 of the Contract,[2] the due date for payment was 7 July 2023. BHC's gross valuation was £3,002,530.00 and, when retention and previous payments were accounted for, the net sum claimed was £564,573.80.

    (ii) W&M's Payment Notice was required to be served on or before 12 July 2023 pursuant to clause 4.7.5, but it was not served until 14 July 2023 under cover of an email from Ms Helena Brown of W&M. The Payment Notice comprised W&M's covering letter dated 14 July 2023, its Payment Certificate and Interim Valuation 13, both setting out a gross valuation of £2,761,812.87 and a net sum due of £243,490.60, and W&M's spreadsheet providing a breakdown of its gross valuation.

    (iii) As such, W&M's Payment Notice was served out of time and, subject to the issue of a valid Pay Less Notice, under clause 4.9.3 JGD was therefore obliged to pay the sum stated as due in IPA13.

2 For the avoidance of doubt, I acknowledge that both parties have referred to the relevant provisions of the Housing Grant, Construction and Regeneration Act 1998 (as amended) (HGCRA) as well, but, unless the context requires otherwise, for brevity I will simply refer to the relevant provisions of the Contract.

(iv) Pursuant to clause 4.9.5 W&M was required to serve a Pay Less Notice no later than 30 July 2023. Under cover of W&M's email timed at 18:00 on 26 July 2023 it provided 'a copy of the Pay Less Notice relating to Valuation 13 reducing the sum payable in the period to £142,529.84'. JGD paid the sum of £142,529.84 by the final date for payment, 4 August 2023.

14. BHC contends that W&M's purported Pay Less Notice dated 26 July 2023 is defective in a number of respects, as follows.

(i) BHC says that pursuant to clause 4.9.5.1 a Pay Less Notice is served where 'the Employer intends to pay less than the sum stated as due from him in a Payment Notice or Interim Payment Application', but that W&M's purported Pay Less Notice merely states that JGD intends to 'deduct from the amount proposed to be made in respect of your Valuation No. 13 and from any sum due under the Building Contract the amount of £100,960.76 comprised of the sums and amounts set out below'. BHC submits that W&M's purported Pay Less Notice therefore does not comply with the requirements of clause 4.9.5.1.

(ii) BHC submits that W&M's purported Pay Less Notice fails to comply with the requirements of clause 4.10.1 because it does not 'specify the sum he considers to be due to the other party at the date the notice is given'. Rather, BHC says that the purported Pay Less Notice is 'doing some other unclear and unspecified exercise', and it is unclear what the words 'amount proposed to be made' mean. Furthermore, BHC argues that it is unclear who was proposing to make the payment and when, and it questions what the words 'and from any sum due under the Building Contract' mean.

(iii) The purported Pay Less Notice sets out two deductions, namely £81,173.26 for a reduction of the preliminaries as a result of delays and £22,910.00 for a reduction in the value of facing brickwork due to 'non-compliant precast units'. There is also a corresponding adjustment of £3,122.50 for retention. BHC contends that the 'provenance and calculation' of the sums of £81,173.26 and £22,910.00, together with the sum stated as due, £142,529.84, are not set out, and, as such, 'there is no basis of calculation' as required by clause 4.10.1.

(iv) BHC submits that the Pay Less Notice appears to cross refer to W&M's Payment Notice, but, as the Payment Notice was late and invalid, it cannot contain 'the sum stated as due from him in a Payment Notice'. As such, BHC submits that this invalidates the Pay Less Notice.

15. As a result of JGD failing to serve a valid Payment Notice and/or Pay Less Notice, BHC contends that JGD should have paid the sum of £564,573.80 by the final date for payment of 4 August 2023, and that JGD is in breach of the Contract by failing to do so. However, BHC acknowledges that since the issue of IPA13, JGD has paid the further sum of £87,587.58, and therefore BHC claims payment of the sum of £476,986.22 in this adjudication. I note that BHC takes no account of the sum of £142,529.84 paid on 4 August 2023.

16. JGD maintains that W&M's Pay Less Notice was valid, and contends that as such BHC was not entitled to payment of the sum stated as due in IPA13, adjusted to take account of subsequent payments, by the final date for payment of 4 August 2023. JGD refers me to the requirements of section 111(4) of the Housing Grants, Construction and Regeneration Act 1996 (as amended) ('the HGCRA'), which sets out materially the same requirements as clause 4.10.1 of the Contract, and submits that the HGCRA says nothing further in respect of the precise information which should be included in a Pay Less Notice.

17. JGD also refers me to the judgment of Coulson J (as he was then) in *Grove Developments Ltd v S&T (UK) Ltd* ([2018] EWHC 123 (TCC)), where he found that there was nothing objectionable in a Pay Less Notice referring back to another clearly identified document. JGD submits that Coulson J identified three key tests for the interpretation of Pay Less Notices:

'(1) How would a "reasonable recipient" have understood the notice.
(2) It is inappropriate to apply a "fine contextual analysis" to the contents of pay less notices and "artificial and contrived" arguments are not allowed.
(3) Does the notice provide an adequate agenda for adjudication.'

18. JGD contends that BHC's objections to the validity of W&M's Pay Less Notice are 'as contrived as they are artificial', and suggests that BHC has failed to account for the contextual background against which the Pay Less Notice was served.

19. BHC also relies on Coulson J's judgment in *Grove v S&T* (TCC), as well as the Court of Appeal's judgment in *S&T (UK) Ltd v Grove Developments Ltd* ([2018] EWCA Civ 2448).

20. It is convenient for me to consider the validity of W&M's Pay Less Notice against the background of BHC's criticisms.

BHC's first criticism: W&M's Pay Less Notice does not comply with clause 4.9.5.1

21. I reject BHC's first criticism of W&M's Pay Less Notice, namely that it has not been served where 'the Employer intends to pay less than the sum stated as due from him in a Payment Notice or Interim Payment Application' as set out in clause 4.9.5.1. I have reached this conclusion for the following reasons.

(i) W&M's Pay Less Notice states that JGD intended to 'deduct from the amount proposed to be made in respect of your Valuation No. 13 and from any sum due under the Building Contract the amount of £100,960.76', and W&M's covering email states that it was attaching 'a copy of the Pay Less Notice relating to Valuation 13 reducing the sum payable in the period to £142,529.84'. It is therefore clear that JGD intended to 'pay less than the sum stated as due from him in a Payment Notice or Interim Payment Application'.

(ii) In any event, clause 4.9.5.1 is simply referring to when a Pay Less Notice should be issued, and it does not set out the requirements of a Pay Less Notice. Rather the only requirements are set out in clause 4.10.1, namely that the Pay Less Notice 'shall specify the sum he considers to be due to the other Party at the date the notice is given and the basis on which that sum has been calculated'.

BHC's second criticism: W&M's Pay Less Notice does not comply with first requirement of clause 4.10.1

22. W&M's Pay Less Notice clearly sets out the sum that JGD considered due to BHC at the date of the notice, namely the sum of £142,529.84, and this is prima facie evidence that W&M's Pay Less Notice meets the first requirement of clause 4.10.1, namely to specify the sum it considered to be due to BHC at the date of the notice. Furthermore:

    (i) I acknowledge that when the statement 'the amount proposed to be made in respect of your Valuation No. 13 and from any sum due under the Building Contract' is read in isolation, there is arguably some uncertainty. However, when the Pay Less Notice is read as a whole it is clear that W&M was referring to a deduction from its Payment Notice dated 14 July 2023. In particular:

        (a) The Pay Less Notice expressly states 'on the valuation works valued in accordance with Notification for Payment Number 13'. Although as a matter of fact none of the documents comprising the Payment Notice were attached to the Pay Less Notice, when considered against the contextual background I am content that the reasonable recipient would have understood that W&M was referring to its assessment issued on 14 July 2023, not least because the sum total of the deduction of £100,960.76 and sum stated as due of £142,529.84 is £243,490.60, which is the sum stated as due in the relevant documents comprising the Payment Notice.

        (b) BHC has made much in the Reply of the different document references in W&M's email of 14 July 2023 and letter of the same date concerning the Payment Notice, as well as the names of the documents actually attached to W&M's email. However, I do not consider that this gets BHC anywhere for two reasons. Firstly, I am content that the reasonable recipient could have worked out what each of the documents were by applying common sense. Secondly, nothing turns on whether the words 'Notification for Payment Number 13' in the Pay Less Notice were referring to W&M's Payment Certificate or Interim Valuation 13 because they both refer to a net sum due of £243,490.60. Furthermore, the spreadsheet valuation attached to the Payment Notice refers to W&M's corresponding gross valuation of £2,761,812.87.

(c) Adopting the language of Coulson J in *Grove v S&T* (TCC), I am therefore content that W&M's calculation and its reference back to its previous calculation would have 'permitted the reasonable recipient to understand precisely' how W&M's valuation was calculated.

(ii) I do not accept that there is any merit in the other elements of BHC's second criticism for the following reasons.

(a) There can be no doubt that W&M's Pay Less Notice was referring to the amount proposed to be paid by JGD. As JGD rightly notes: 'Who else would be making payment of a positive amount to BHC?'

(b) The Contract does not require a Pay Less Notice to set out the date when the payment is to be made, and the final date for payment is 28 days after its due date in accordance with clause 4.9.1.

(c) Nothing turns on the use of the word 'made' rather than 'paid', and its meaning would be obvious to the reasonable recipient of W&M's Pay Less Notice.

(d) The words 'and from any sum due under the Building Contract' were evidently superfluous, but their inclusion does not invalidate the Pay Less Notice which otherwise complies with the requirements of clause 4.10.1.

(e) I do not accept that these issues 'paint a picture of confusion and uncertainty' as alleged by BHC.

BHC's third criticism: the 'provenance and calculation' of the sums of £81,173.26, £22,910.00 and £142,529.84 is not set out

23. I am content that the Pay Less Notice also complies with the second requirement of clause 4.10.2 because it sets out the basis on which that sum was calculated. In particular:

(i) The lack of a breakdown of the sums of £81,173.26 and £22,910.00 set out in W&M's Pay Less Notice is arguably the high point of BHC's case, but on balance I am not persuaded that any such breakdown was required for the following reasons.

(a) Nowhere in clause 4.10.1 does it state that it is necessary for the calculations in Pay Less Notices to be set out with any specific degree of granularity.

(b) The Pay Less Notice sets out an explanation for the grounds of each deduction, and BHC was evidently aware of the fact that there would be an extended date for completion. The issue of the allegedly defective precast units was also clearly known to BHC and expressly referred to in a letter of non-compliance issued by W&M on 12 July 2023.

(ii) As set out above, the basis on which the sum of £142,529.84 had been calculated is clear once account is taken of W&M's Payment Notice.

(iii) That W&M's Pay Less Notice set out the basis on which the sum due had been calculated is evident when the test set out by Coulson J in *Grove v S&T* (TCC) is applied, namely: 'One way of testing whether the contents of the notice are adequate is to see if the notice provides an adequate agenda for a dispute about valuation and/or any cross claims available to the employer.' Taking account of my findings above, I am in no doubt that W&M's Pay Less Notice would provide such an agenda because the disputed items of the measured works were clearly set out in the spreadsheet valuation attached to W&M's Payment Notice, and the two other disputed issues, namely the reduction in the preliminaries due to the extended contract duration and the reduction in the value of the facing brickwork, were set out in the Pay Less Notice and known to BHC.

BHC's fourth criticism: W&M's Pay Less Notice cross refers to W&M's invalid Payment Notice

24. I do not accept that the Pay Less Notice is invalid because it cross refers to a Payment Notice that is itself invalid. I have reached this conclusion for the following reasons.

    (i) Clause 4.9.5.1 states that where 'the Employer intends to pay less than the sum stated as due from him in a Payment Notice or Interim Payment Application', he is to serve a Pay Less Notice. JGD clearly intended to pay less than the sum stated in IPA13, and W&M has therefore served a Pay Less Notice. The fact that the sum due has been calculated by reference to an invalid Payment Notice does not affect its intention to pay less than the sum stated as due in IPA13.

    (ii) To the extent that BHC is contending that it is not permissible for a Pay Less Notice to cross refer to a document that is invalid, I do not accept that contention. I agree with JGD that the validity of the document cross referred to is not relevant, and it cannot in itself invalidate a Pay Less Notice. Indeed, in *Grove v S&T* (TCC) the court found that cross referencing to a spreadsheet attached to an invalid Payment Notice did not invalidate the relevant Pay Less Notice.

Summary – Issue 1

25. I have rejected all of BHC's criticisms of W&M's Pay Less Notice. W&M's Pay Less Notice was issued on time, and I am content that

it adequately specified the sum it considered to be due to BHC and the basis on which that sum had been calculated. I therefore find that it constitutes an effective Pay Less Notice under the Contract and HGCRA, and it follows that

(i) BHC was not entitled to the sum stated as due in IPA13, £564,573.80, by the final date for payment of 4 August 2023, and nor is it now entitled to the sum of £476,986.22 in this adjudication;

(ii) JGD is not in breach of the Contract by not paying BHC the sum stated as due in IPA13 (as adjusted) by the final date for payment, 4 August 2023 – rather, JGD was obliged to pay the sum stated as due in W&M's Pay Less Notice, £142,529.84, and it duly did so.

26. I therefore find that BHC is not entitled to payment in this adjudication.

27. **Finding – Issue 1. Accordingly, I find that BHC is not entitled to payment in this adjudication.**

ISSUE 2. IS BHC ENTITLED TO INTEREST AND, IF SO, HOW MUCH?

28. I have found that BHC is not entitled to payment in this adjudication and it therefore follows that I find that it is not entitled to interest.

29. **Finding – Issue 2. Accordingly, I find that BHC is not entitled to interest.**

MY FEES AND EXPENSES

30. BHC has been unsuccessful in this matter. Therefore, notwithstanding the parties' ongoing joint and several liability for my fees, BHC shall be primarily liable for my fees and expenses in their entirety.

DECLARATIONS AND DIRECTIONS

Having regard to my findings above and the relief sought, I decide as follows:

1. JGD is not in breach of the Contract by not paying BHC the sum stated as due in IPA13 (as adjusted) by the final date for payment of 4 August 2023.

2. BHC is not entitled to payment in this adjudication.

3. BHC is not entitled to interest.

4. BHC shall be primarily liable for my fees and expenses in the sum of £3,675.00 plus VAT of £735.00 making a total of £4,410.00 in accordance with the invoice I have issued. Until payment in full has been received in respect of my fees and expenses, the parties shall remain jointly and severally liable for all fees and expenses incurred by me pursuant to this adjudication, together with any accruable interest. I will inform the parties when this liability has been discharged.

Reached this 4 October 2023

Thomas Marks

Mr Thomas Marks
MCMS Limited
45 Tabernacle Street
London
EC2A 4AA

APPENDIX C

Example adjudicator's schedule: variations

VO Ref	DDL	FML	Adjudi-cator	Adjudicator's comments
001	£15,460.15	£15,460.15	£15,460.15	Not in dispute.
002	£447.41	£447.41	£447.41	Not in dispute.
003	£1,218.74	£1,218.74	£1,218.74	Not in dispute.
005	£762.47	£471.72	£658.55	I find that the correct value of VO 005 is £658.55 because: (1) On balance, given the nature of the works in question, and the need to work around other trades on a completed installation, I accept that two operatives would be required, plus a supervisor. I also consider that the time allowed by DDL is reasonable notwithstanding that the daywork sheet is not signed. However, I agree with FML that a skilled operative and a mate would have sufficed, and that it should have been possible to test the pipework within the time allowed. I therefore adjust Mr Wilkinson's rate to £25.00/hr and find that the correct value of the labour is £397.00 (2hrs x £40.00/hr + 6hrs x £32.00/hr + 5hrs x £25.00/hr). (2) Although FML has complained about DDL's valuation of materials at 40% of the rates in the Schedule of Rates, it has nevertheless adopted DDL's valuation and added overheads and profit (OH&P) of 15%. I therefore adopt FML's valuation of the materials, £100.04 (£86.99 + £13.05). (3) Although I acknowledge that DDL has not provided the Prime Cost of the plant and has also wrongly included for hand tools, FML's valuation makes no allowance for other plant set out in DDL's daywork sheet, which I accept would have been required for the work in question. I therefore consider a valuation of £45.00 to be reasonable, plus 15% OH&P resulting in a total of £51.75 for the plant. (4) FML has added 20% for preliminaries, which I accept is reasonable and I therefore adopt it. I therefore find that the correct value of VO 005 is £658.55 ((£397.00 + £100.04 + £51.75) + 20%).
006	£420.13	£420.13	£420.13	Not in dispute.
007	£15,382.62	£15,382.62	£15,382.62	Not in dispute.

VO Ref	DDL	FML	Adjudicator	Adjudicator's comments
008	£784.76	£315.80	£714.10	I find that the correct value of VO 008 is £714.10 because: (1) For the same reasons as VO 005 I adopt DDL's valuation of the labour and adjust the rate of one of the skilled operatives to £25.00/hr to account for the fact that a skilled operative and mate would have sufficed. I also make no separate allowance for the testing. I therefore find that the correct value of the labour is £536.00 (2hrs x £40.00/hr + 8hrs x £32.00/hr + 8hrs x £25.00/hr). (2) I consider that DDL's valuation of the materials is reasonable, and I note that FML has adopted the same manner of valuing the materials. I add 15% OH&P for the reasons set out in the main body of my Decision, and I therefore find that the correct value of the materials is £30.33 (£26.37 + 15%). (3) I allow 50% of DDL's valuation of the plant, and add 15% for OH&P for the reasons set out in the main body of my Decision. I therefore find that the correct value of the plant is £28.75 (£25.00 + 15%). (4) Adding 20% for preliminaries, I therefore find that the correct value of VO 008 is £714.10 ((£536.00 + £30.33 + £28.75) + 20%).
010	£9,252.21	£8,381.86	£8,381.86	I adopt FML's valuation of VO 010 because: (1) The work evidently involved the extension of the pipework to the location where the TMVs would be installed, and I agree with FML that this work can be properly valued by measurement and the application of the rates and prices in the Sub-Subcontract, namely those in the Schedule of Rates. (2) I accept that FML's measured valuation is reasonable given the works involved, and it has evidently used the appropriate rates. I therefore adopt FML's measured valuation.
011	£1,731.68	£0.00	£1,568.40	On balance, I am persuaded that VO 011 constitutes a variation because, as rightly noted by DDL, it had no design and/or coordination responsibilities under the Sub-Subcontract. Furthermore, while I note the contents of ND2, DDL evidently installed the pipework at the height on the design drawings and FML has not demonstrated that the clash with the ceilings could have been identified from the drawings. I find that the correct value of VO 011 is £1,568.40 because: (1) For the same reasons as VO 005 I adopt DDL's valuation of the labour and adjust the rate of one of the skilled operatives to £25.00/hr to account for the fact that a skilled operative and mate would have sufficed. I also make no separate allowance for the testing. I therefore find that the correct value of the labour is £1,106.00 (2hrs x £40.00/hr + 18hrs x £32.00/hr + 18hrs x £25.00/hr). (2) I consider that DDL's valuation of the materials is reasonable, and I note that FML has adopted the same manner of valuing the materials. I add 15% OH&P for the reasons set out in the main body of my Decision, and I therefore find that the correct value of the materials is £149.25 (£129.78 + 15%). (3) I allow 50% of DDL's valuation of the plant, and add 15% for OH&P for the reasons set out in the main body of my Decision. I therefore find that the correct value of the plant is £51.75 (£45.00 + 15%). (4) Adding 20% for preliminaries I therefore find that the correct value of VO 011 is £1,568.40 ((£1,106.00 + £149.25 + £51.75) + 20%).

VO Ref	DDL	FML	Adjudi-cator	Adjudicator's comments
012	£13,200.85	£0.00	£12,779.52	On balance, I am persuaded that VO 012 constitutes a variation because: (A) Notwithstanding what was indicated on the Contract drawings, it is clear from point 17 of DDL's tender clarifications, which formed part of the Sub-Subcontract, that DDL had assumed that the FCU's would be supplied with internal air vents via the dominator set, and it had therefore made no allowance for air vents. I consider that a reasonable person with all the background knowledge of the parties would understand that the parties intended the air vents to be excluded. (B) DDL had no design responsibility and I therefore do not accept that the fact that pipework was shown as higher than FCUs is relevant, particularly where the air vents had been specifically excluded in the Sub-Subcontract. (C) There is no evidence to support FML's contention that the FCUs referred to by DDL are landlord's FCUs, or that DDL has priced the wrong works. Furthermore, in circumstances where no design for the air vents was provided to DDL, I do not accept that its installation was not efficient or cost effective. I find that the correct value of VO 012 is £12,779.52 because: (1) DDL has evidently valued VO 012 on a measurement basis using the rates in the Schedule of Rates in accordance with clause 17.2. I agree with DDL that the work can be measured under clause 17.2 and I therefore accept that it has adopted the correct method of valuation. (2) DDL has used the appropriate rates for the YP24 and VP6 fittings from the Schedule of Rates, but does not appear to have used the appropriate rate for the coupling, namely £7.34 (YP1). No rates are included for the ARVs in the Schedule of Rates, but I consider DDL's allowance of £58.36 to be reasonable. The appropriate rate per FCU is therefore £163.84 ((£11.21 + £7.82 + £7.34 + £14.59) x 4no.), and multiplied by 65 FCUs this results in a total of £10,649.60. I make no allowance for sundries as I consider that these would be included in the aforesaid rates. (3) Taking account of the 20% addition for preliminaries, I therefore find that the correct value of VO 012 is £12,779.52 (£10,649.60 + 20%).
013	£1,447.00	£0.00	£1,447.00	On balance, I am persuaded that VO 013 constitutes a variation. I have reached this conclusion because, although I note the requirement in Numbered Document 8 (ND8) of the Sub-Subcontract for DDL to undertake the setting out, the location of the shower mixers was clearly predetermined as they were to be installed on pattresses installed by others, and DDL was not required to undertake any setting out. FML has also not demonstrated how DDL failed in the setting-out of the mixers. DDL has not provided a breakdown of its revised valuation included in the Reply, but on balance I consider that it is reasonable given the nature and extent of the relocation works and I therefore adopt it.

VO Ref	DDL	FML	Adjudicator	Adjudicator's comments
014	£583.77	£145.44	£504.83	I find that the correct value of VO 014 is £504.83 because: (1) On balance, given the revisit nature of the works and the need to work around other services, etc., I agree with DDL that it is not appropriate to value them by measurement, and that it should therefore be valued on the basis of the labour, materials and plant used. (2) I consider that DDL's labour allowance is reasonable, but I make no separate allowance for the testing as there is no evidence that the original pipework had been tested as noted by FML. I therefore find that the correct value of the labour is £328.00. (3) I consider that DDL's valuation of the materials is reasonable, and I note that FML has adopted the same manner of valuing the materials. I add 15% OH&P for the reasons set out in the main body of my Decision and I therefore find that the correct value of the materials is £40.94 (£35.60 + 15%). (4) I allow 50% of DDL's valuation of the plant, and add 15% for OH&P for the reasons set out in the main body of my Decision. I therefore find that the correct value of the plant is £51.75 (£45.00 + 15%). (5) Adding 20% for preliminaries I therefore find that the correct value of VO 014 is £504.83 ((£328.00 + £40.94 + £51.75) + 20%).
015	£6,019.20	£6,019.20	£6,019.20	Not in dispute.
016	£1,280.16	£431.09	£819.44	I find that the correct value of VO 015 is £819.44 because: (1) While I accept that this was a complex relocation around existing services that would have taken more than one day, I do not accept that it would have taken two skilled operatives and one PM 9hrs. DDL criticises FML for not providing a 'time and motion study' but fails to provide one of its own. I consider 2hrs for a PM and 9hrs for a skilled operative and mate to be reasonable, including the testing, resulting in a valuation of £593.00 for the labour (2hrs x £40.00/hr + 9hrs x £32.00/hr + 9hrs x £25.00/hr). (2) I consider that DDL's valuation of the materials is reasonable, and I add 15% OH&P for the reasons set out in the main body of my Decision. I therefore find that the correct value of the materials is £38.12 (£33.15 + 15%). (3) I allow 50% of DDL's valuation of the plant, and add 15% for OH&P for the reasons set out in the main body of my Decision. I therefore find that the correct value of the plant is £51.75 (£45.00 + 15%). (4) Adding 20% for preliminaries, I therefore find that the correct value of VO 014 is £819.44 ((£593.00 + £38.12 + £51.75) + 20%).
Variations total	**£67,991.15**	**£48,694.16**	**£65,821.95**	

APPENDIX D

Example submissions schedule

BENNET CONSTRUCTION PLC V MERYTON HOMES – SUBMISSIONS SCHEDULE

Issues

(i) What is the correct assessment of the Compensation Event Delay to planned Completion, and what is the resulting revised Completion Date?

(a) Did DE02 delay planned Completion and, if so, by how long?
(b) Did DE03 delay planned Completion and, if so, by how long?
(c) Did DE04 delay planned Completion and, if so, by how long?
(d) Did DE05 delay planned Completion and, if so, by how long?

(ii) What is the correct assessment of the Bennet Preliminaries?

(iii) Is either party entitled to payment in this adjudication and, if so, how much?

(iv) Is Bennet entitled to interest and, if so, how much?

Issue	Referral	Response	Reply	Rejoinder	Surrejoinder
(1) EoT generally	• PM instructed Bennet not to submit Cl32 progs: Ref para 11.4–11.5, 25–28, Bingley report para 1.7–1.8, 8.9, 9.1–9.14, Wickham WS para 22–24, Lucas WS para 19–31 • Time-slice – retro analysis – stages: Ref para 29–34, Bingley report para 1.11–1.18, 10.1–10.8, 11.1–11.13, 12.1–12.9, 31.1–31.14 • Baseline/planned intent: Bingley para 14.1–14.13, Wickham WS para 25–53 • Summary of delays & stages: Ref para 35–40, Bingley report para 1.19–1.35	• PM did not instruct Cl32 progs to cease: Res para 40–45, 54–62, Darcy report para 2.3.1–2.3.7, 3.1–3.15, Collins WS para 12–16, 22–24 • Time-slice – retro analysis – stages - summary: Res para 68–116, Darcy report para 4.1–4.10 (TS don't show CP)	• Lack of HE evidence: Rep para 1.5, 2.3–2.4 • No prog analysis & Darcy errors: Rep para 1.8–1.9, Bingley para 1.3–1.8 • Cl32 progs: Rep para 1.7, 1.7.1–1.7.3, 3.10–3.11, 3.14–3.15, Bingley report para 2.1–2.11 • Time-slice, etc.: Bingley para 3.1–3.21 (TS does show CP), 5.1–5.5	• No prog analysis irrelevant: Rej para 6 • Cl32 progs: Rej para 7–11, 57–59 • Time-slice, etc.: Rej para 17.1–17.8, Darcy report para 3.1.1–3.1.18, 3.2.1–3.2.16	• Lack of HE evidence: Sur para 1.4–1.5 • Cl32 progs: Sur para 2 • Time-slice, etc.: Bingley report para 3.1–3.10, 4.1–4.11, 6.1–6.3
(1a) DE02 – Meryton House	• DE02 Meryton House: Ref para 38.2, DE02 narrative, Bingley report para 16.1–16.22, 23.1–23.4, 24.1–24.30 (TS1), 30.3–30.4, Wickham WS para 120–144, Lucas WS para 10–18	• DE02 Meryton House: Res para 72–74, Darcy report para 2.2.1, 5.1–5.5	• DE02 Meryton House: Rep para 3.18–3.21, Bingley report para 4.5–4.9	• DE02 Meryton House: Rej para 19, Darcy report para 3.4.1–3.4.6	• DE02 Meryton House: Sur para 6, Bingley Report para 5.1–5.5
(1b) DE03 – Earth-works	• DE03 Earthworks: Ref para 38.3, DE03 narrative, Bingley report para 17.1–17.26, 25.1–25.37 (TS2), 30.5–30.7, Wickham WS para 145–175	• DE03 Earthworks: Res para 75–76, Darcy report para 2.2.1, 5.6	• DE03 Earthworks: Rep para 3.22–3.24, Bingley para 4.10–4.14	• DE03 Earthworks: Rej para 20, Darcy report para 3.5.1–3.5.5	• DE03 Earthworks: Sur para 7, Bingley Report para 5.6–5.14
(1c) DE04 – Dashwood building	• DE04 Dashwood building: Ref para 38.4, DE04 narrative, Bingley report para 18.1–18.23, 25.1–25.37 (TS2), 30.8–30.11, Wickham WS para 176–196	• DE04 Dashwood building: Res para 77–80, Darcy report para 2.2.1, 5.7	• DE04 Dashwood building: Rep para 3.25–3.27, Bingley para 4.15–4.21	• DE04 Dashwood building: Rej para 21, Darcy report para 3.6.1–3.6.7	• DE04 Dashwood building: Sur para 7, Bingley Report para 5.6–5.14

Issue	Referral	Response	Reply	Rejoinder	Surrejoinder
(1d) DE05 – Water main	• DE05 Water main: Ref para 38.5, DE05 narrative, Bingley report para 19.1–19.57, 26.1–26.30 (TS3), 27.1–27.25 (TS4), 30.12–30.15, Wickham WS para 61–68, 76–78 83–86, 197–265	• DE05 Water main: Res para 83–90, 91–98, Darcy report para 2.3.6–2.3.7, 6.1–6.6	• DE05 Water main: Rep para 3.28–3.30, Bingley para 4.22–4.33	• DE05 Water main: Rej para 22 and 23, Darcy report para 2.1.5–2.1.9, 3.8.1–3.8.8, 3.9.1–3.9.5	• DE05 Water main: Sur para 8, Bingley Report para 5.15–5.19
(2) Bennet prelims	• Prelims generally: Ref para 13.5–13.10, 14.1–14.5, 42–47, Lucas WS para 24–32, Gardiner WS para 10–68	• Prelims generally: Res para 119–163	• Prelims generally: Rep para 1.11, 2.6–2.8, 3.41–3.59	• Prelims generally: Rej para 27, 32–53, 61–62	• Prelims generally: Sur para 11–17
Error 1: Brandons		• Error 1: Res para 133–134	• Error 1: Rep para 3.41.1, 3.44–3.45	• Error 1: Rej para 34–35	• Error 1: Sur para 11.1–11.3
Error 2: Bennet owned		• Error 2: Res para 143.1	• Error 2: Rep para 3.41.2, 3.51–3.54	• Error 2: Rej para 36–39	• Error 2: Sur para 12.1–12.2
Error 3: Bennet hired		• Error 3: Res para 143.2, 144–155	• Error 3: Rep para 3.41.3, 3.51–3.54	• Error 3: Rej para 40–44	• Error 3: Sur para 13.1–13.6, 14.1
Error 4: COVID		• Error 4: Res para 142	• Error 4: Rep para 3.41.4, 3.50	• Error 4: Rej para 45–47	• Error 4: Sur para 15.1–15.4
Error 5: Sleeper		• Error 5: Res para 136, 156–158	• Error 5: Rep para 3.41.5, 3.47, 3.55–3.56	• Error 5: Rej para 48–52	• Error 5: Sur para 16.1–16.2
Error 6: Tender rates		• Error 6: See hire above	• Error 6: Rep para 3.41.6	• Error 6: Rej para 38	• Error 6: Sur para 17.1
(3) Payment			• Figures previously paid: Rep para 3.7		
(4) Interest	• Interest: Ref para 48–49, Gardiner WS para 69–85	• Interest: Res para 164–165			

Index

N

O

P

Q

R

S

T

U

V

W

LEGISLATION

Australia

Canada

Hong Kong

Ireland

Isle of Man

Malaysia

Mauritius

New Zealand

Singapore

South Africa

Thailand

United Kingdom

CASE LAW